Dare to Dream Again

Dare to Dream Again

Getting Back Up When Life Knocks You Down

Jeff Chacon

DPI

DISCIPLESHIP
PUBLICATIONS
INTERNATIONAL

Dare to Dream Again

© 2004 by Discipleship Publications International

2 Sterling Road

Billerica, Massachusetts 01862

Original poetry © Jeff Chacon.

Original poetry © Kim Pullen.

Printed in the United States of America

The "NIV" and "New International Version" trademarks are registered in the United States Patent Trademark Office by the International Bible Society. Use of either trademark requires the permission of the International Bible Society.

ISBN: 1-57782-194-7

Cover Design: Brian Branch
Interior Design: Thais Gloor

To Tyler, Kyle and Ryan,

Tonight Kyle asked if you boys were in the book. I said, "No, come to think of it, you're not. But I will dedicate it to you."

As I've thought more about it, I realize I should have said that you were all through the book. Because when I wrote it, I thought about you guys—all three of you—the whole time. And that's the truth. Everything I am, I dream about, and I do—I do it for you, your momma and for God, because I love you three boys, your momma, and Him, more than life itself.

Don't ever forget that.

Love forever,
Dad

CONTENTS

FOREWORD
Dare to Dream Again

One thing is certain: my life has been changed, and changed repeatedly, by the books I have been blessed to read. Reading spiritual books is just another way of being instructed and inspired by a gifted teacher whose heart has been stirred by God to the point that he must share it with others. Jeff Chacon clearly has experienced such a heart-stirring by God, as you will discover when reading this book.

Often, when you read a new book, you ask the question: "Is the author the 'real deal'?" Most of us have become a little cynical when reading books of the self-help genre, for we have heard too many stories about authors who write well but live poorly. They "talk the talk," but they don't "walk the walk." The best part of writing this foreword is that I have as much respect for Jeff Chacon as I do for any man I know.

In 1985 when I became the lead evangelist for the San Diego Church of Christ, Jeff was a neophyte ministry intern with a heart full of dreams and a gleam in his eye. I was privileged to see him get engaged to his girlfriend, Lisa, to marry her, and to start their family. I have watched them mature through the years, as God's hand in their lives led them through valleys and up to mountaintops. I know of no man with whom I agree more on his understanding of how the God of the Bible should be viewed and followed in the daily life of a disciple of Jesus, and I know no man who better practices what he preaches—praise Jesus for that!

When beginning a new book, we are eager to check out the content and writing style. Some books have good content, but are not very interesting to read. Others hold your interest wonderfully well, but are shallow at best and inaccurate at worst. With excellent content on a much-needed topic and a style that compels you to keep reading once you start, Jeff hits a home run on both counts.

Jeff is a dreamer; this is shown by many things, not the least of which is a childlike maturity. He writes as a seasoned disciple, but with a youthful zest for life that comes through clearly. I also see his dreamer's personality evidenced in his flair for poetry. Jeff's poems are interspersed throughout the book, as are those of others. Time and again, he poignantly describes the challenge of remaining a dreamer when, as the song in *Les Miserables* puts it, "life has killed the dream I dreamed." Jeff makes it clear that God never designed this life to be "fun in the sun," but rather "maturing in the Son." The difference in these two views is so great that only he who sees life from God's perspective will be able to keep dreaming through the ups and downs of life. Thank the Lord that in this book, Jeff helps us take hold of God's perspective!

—Gordon Ferguson

It is not the critic who counts,
nor the man who points out how the strong man stumbled,
or where the doer of deeds could have done better.
The credit belongs to the man who is actually in the arena,
whose face is marred by dust, and sweat, and blood;
who strives valiantly; who errs and comes short again and again;
who knows great enthusiasms, great devotions,
who spends himself in a worthy cause;
who, at the best, knows in the end the triumph of high achievement,
and who, if he fails, at least fails while daring greatly,
so that his place shall never be with those cold and timid souls
who know neither victory nor defeat.

—Theodore Roosevelt

INTRODUCTION
Dare to Dream Again

I'll never forget that night. My wife and I had gone out on a Saturday night to a small dinner playhouse a few miles from our house in one of the eastern suburbs of Denver. What I didn't know is that my heart would be unexpectedly ripped out of my chest and laid bare for everyone to see before the night was over. I would be exposed for the dreamer that I am, as the theme of my life would be acted out on the stage before me...

An Impossible Dream

The performance that night was an adapted presentation of the classic Spanish drama, Don Quixote, written by Miguel de Cervantes in 1605. It is a classic tale of dreams, dreamers and their adversaries. One man dares to dream an impossible dream, and those around him are never the same again.

The story begins with a common country squire named Alonso Quijana. He is an aging, retired school teacher who loves to read books about chivalry and gallantry; they fill him with the breath of heaven and make him feel that life is worth living. The valiant books are inviting to the point of being painful. One day, when he can stand the pain of conformity and mediocrity no longer, the adventurous old man dares to imagine himself as what he has always dreamed of becoming: a noble knight who bravely lives for the good and courageously rights all wrongs. From that point on, he dubs himself "Don Quixote de La Mancha"!

The old man with the new vision sets out for adventure, taking his faithful servant, Sancho, with him. Loyal Sancho, though not really sure if the old man is in his right mind, is somehow captivated and stirred by the visionary's dream.

After battling windmills and other imaginary foes, the two fanciful travelers soon come upon a country tavern and enter, seeking a place to stay for the night. There they meet the unlikely character that will rip both the hero and the audience's hearts out forevermore. She is simply known as Aldonza, a woman who has forgotten she is a lady, between her day job as cook and her night job as any man's mistress. She's a lost soul who doesn't feel anything in a heart that long ago has ceased to beat with love or life.

Enter the dreamer. The old man with the hot vision sets his magical eyes on her and sees not a country harlot, but a woman of immeasurable value and worth. He asks her name, and when she retorts that it is "Aldonza," he looks into her eyes and tells her that her true name is one that mortals dare not speak, and angels only whisper: "Dulcinea."

The peculiar self-proclaimed knight has renamed her. In the eyes of this beholder, she is no longer a common harlot with no love or life in her heart, but the original version of her, the sweet virgin and beautiful lady, Dulcinea (which in Spanish has the sense of "sweetheart," and as a result of this classic in Spanish literature, has come to mean "lady love" or "she of whom one dreams").

But the transformation does not come easily. Aldonza does not see what the dreamer sees in her. She is initially perturbed by this foolish game he seems to be playing with her and is suspicious of his motives.

But Don Quixote tells her that he is a noble man who seeks only to follow the quest of his heart.

The wounded and jaded tavern maid spits on the floor beside him and tells him what she thinks of his quest, marching away in disgust. But then for some unknown reason, slowly, and not knowing exactly why, she turns back to him and asks awkwardly, with a faraway hint of hope in her voice, what he means by "quest."

Don Quixote's response is timeless and pure, nobility's soul laid bare, and the anthem of every true dreamer before and since. He speaks of the mission of every true knight to dream an impossible dream, to fight a brave battle, and to live for a glorious cause. That is his quest.

By this time, I'm a complete mess at the dinner table. I'm holding my wife's hand and sobbing uncontrollably, hoping that no one will notice this blubbering fool in the middle of an otherwise dignified dinner theater.

But I don't care. My heart has found expression and my soul has found its anthem. I am that dreamer; that is my quest. It's why I became a Christian more than twenty years ago, and it's the fire that still ignites me today. To dream God's impossible dream, to fight God's brave, eternal battle, and to live for the most glorious cause on earth—this is the quest of every true disciple of Jesus Christ, for it is a description of our Lord's own life and mission.

Visions of Jesus, heroically giving his life for us on the cross come racing to mind. That's whom I want to follow! That's whom I want to be like! That's the life worth living! That's the death worth dying! That's the dream that captured my heart long ago, and that's the dream that still fires me up today: to be like Jesus and make God's dreams come true!

My Name Is Dulcinea

Let's get back to the story of Don Quixote for a moment: it continues, as all good stories do, with the realism of the world violently bursting its way into the hearts and lives of our heroes. After daring to share in a taste of Don Quixote's dream, Aldonza is cruelly raped by a foul group of men right there on the tables of the all-too-familiar walls of her prison home, the country inn. She is robbed of both her dignity and her hope; crushed and crestfallen, she slumps to the floor, a mere shadow of the woman she'd hoped to become.

Don Quixote finds her in this condition and tries awkwardly to comfort her. But Aldonza is full of bitterness and rage, angry now that she ever allowed the eccentric stranger to awaken in her dreams long buried. Yet still he calls her by her heavenly name, "Dulcinea," though she vehemently objects to his lunacy. But the great knight remains undaunted, convinced in his heart of her unblemished beauty.

Then the real horror begins. Don Quixote's niece and a local padre and a doctor arrive at the door to bring the wandering fool back to his senses. Determined to bring the old man back down to earth and to remind him that he is no more than a simple peasant teacher, they have devised a plan whereby they surround him with mirrors, assault his identity, and force him to face reality. At first, the gallant knight fights bravely, shielding his heart from the vicious accusations of "madman" and "pretender" that they hurl at him like stones. But, soon Don Quixote is brought down by the chink in all of our armor: the knowledge of who we are in the flesh; the failures that we all secretly fear ourselves to be.

He is robbed of the hopes and dreams that make his life worth living. Then he is physically beaten almost to the point of death and brought back to his peasant home, under the feigned care of his supposed benefactors.

But all is not lost. It never is.

In the last, climactic scene of the story, Aldonza has sought Don Quixote out and dramatically bursts through the guards and the doors to see him. But the old and dying man does not recognize her.

She begs that he try hard to remember the way that he first looked at her and saw more than a country harlot, the way that he renamed her with a name that she secretly longed for, and now desperately dared to desire. She begged him to speak again the name that even angels only whisper: Dulcinea.

It is the mention of Dulcinea that eventually brings the dying man back to his senses. The song of a life once longed for now stirs his slumbering soul, and beginning to awaken, he sits up in his bed, searching the woman's eyes for more clues as to where this former life has been hidden.

Her eyes wide, she speaks excitedly to him of chivalry, bravery and a quest—to dream an impossible dream, to fight a brave battle, and to live for a glorious cause.

The old man with the renewed vision almost falls out of bed, calling for his armor, his sword and his loyal servant, Sancho. His faithful friend hurries to his side, eager to accompany the roused warrior on more heroic adventures!

But the old man has been beaten badly, and his wounded body will no longer serve his vivid imagination. Collapsing to the ground, he dies in the arms of both his loyal friend and his fair lady.

Deeply saddened, Sancho laments to Aldonza that his beloved master is dead. But the woman boldly interrupts him, assuring him that Don Quixote is not dead as long as his memory lives on, and that her name is not Aldonza…it is Dulcinea!

What Is Your Name?

What is your name? Do you remember? Has it been so long since you dreamed that impossible dream, fought that brave battle, and lived for that glorious cause? Remember what it was like to need only the sword of God's word in one hand, and the shield of faith in the other?

We are more than the sum of our failures.
We are more than our latest defeat.
We were crafted for heavenly glory,
where there still is reserved a seat.

Once all the world was a canvas,
and we held a brush in our hand.
We really believed it was possible:
"Go in and take the land!"

But like with our brother, Don Quixote,
the Evil One has had his way,
thrusting his sword in our sides,
and then calling it a day!

Can't you hear above the crowd,
the One who still calls your name?
How many defeats doesn't matter—
to him it's all the same.

All that matters
is the quest in your heart.
You've got to finish
what you start!

"Get up, O Warrior!"
the angel gallery shouts aloud.
"Take up the sword
and lift your head proud!"

For the fight is not over
until you fail to rise.
Get back up,
and look to the skies!

Your commander still rides,
still faithful and true.
And he's calling your name—
he's calling for you!

—Jeff Chacon

I hope that you hear God encouraging you and calling your name throughout this book.

Whether you've lost a loved one, lost your health or lost your faith; whether you've been in and out of church leadership, in and out of a job, or in and out of love; whether you've seen a leader fall, seen your child fall or seen yourself fall, the pages of this book were meant to be healing balm for your soul.

Through scriptures, songs and stories, I hope that you'll be deeply encouraged by every single page, and that you'll recover the quest that God has placed in your heart.

Never, Never, Never Give Up!

The story is told of a powerful commencement speech delivered by the great British statesman and orator Sir Winston

Churchill to a graduating class of college seniors. Upon Churchill's introduction, the crowd jumped to its feet and vigorously cheered for some time, honoring the man who had heroically inspired the people of Britain to persevere during the darkest days of World War II, until the tide was turned in their hard fought war with Nazi Germany. After the applause subsided, Churchill gave an inspiring speech that included the following oft-quoted lines:

> "Never give in. Never give in. Never, never, never, never—in nothing, great or small, large or petty—never give in, except to convictions of honour and good sense. Never yield to force. Never yield to the apparently overwhelming might of the enemy."

That was the message of Winston Churchill that night. And that is the message of God for us today. No matter how bad it gets, no matter how bad you feel, no matter how far you've fallen: never, never, never give up!

Listen to the inspiring words of Jesus himself to the church in Philadelphia, as recorded by the apostle John in Revelation 3:11–13:

> "I am coming soon. Hold on to what you have, so that no one will take your crown. Him who overcomes I will make a pillar in the temple of my God. Never again will he leave it. I will write on him the name of my God and the name of the city of my God, the new Jerusalem, which is coming down out of heaven from my God; and I will also write on him my new name. He who has an ear, let him hear what the Spirit says to the churches."

Hang on. He's coming soon. Don't let anyone take your crown. Don't let anyone take your name. And don't let anyone take your dreams. Whatever you've been through, however many times you've failed, I beg you—dare to dream again!

Look to the Sky!

I looked at the road
with its potholes and pitfalls
and wondered how I'd get by.
But he reached for my arm
and pointed up high,
and simply said—
"Look to the sky!"

I found myself drowning
in water so deep,
afraid of the waves, so high!
But he reached out his hand
and pulled me back up, saying—
"You forgot to look to the sky."

I looked at the mountains
that loomed before me
and wondered, "Why even try?"
But before I knew it
I was on his back, and he said—
"Let's climb to the sky!"

I looked at the valleys
and saw all my failures,
and that's when I began to cry.
But he lifted my chin,
and said ever so softly—
"You've forgotten why I died."

"I died for your sins
and I died for your failings,
But in the grave I no longer lie.
I've risen from the dead!
There's no reason to cry!
Just remember…to look to the sky!"

—*Jeff Chacon*

1

LOOK TO THE SKY!

God Never Gives Up on Us

What would it take for God to give up on you? How bad does it have to get before God scraps the "you project" and moves on to someone else? Have you slipped beyond God's reach? Is his arm too short to save this time? (Isaiah 59:1). Are you afraid that you've fallen past the point of no return? Has God turned his back on you? Has he forgotten you? Do you sometimes feel that he has forsaken you forever?

Most people feel abandoned by God at some time in their lives. We can feel particularly estranged from God during times of physical or emotional suffering, transition or bereavement. But we can be sure that God is particularly close to us at times like these, for his word assures us that "he heals the broken-hearted and binds up their wounds" (Psalm 147:3).

One of the most common times that we feel distant from God is when we have sinned against him and we are undergoing his discipline. The incomparably vulnerable David shares this painful spiritual experience with us in Psalm 38 when he writes,

> O LORD do not rebuke me in your anger
>   or discipline me in your wrath.
> For your arrows have pierced me,
>   and your hand has come upon me.
> Because of your wrath there is no health in my body;
>   my bones have no soundness because of my sin.

> My guilt has overwhelmed me
> > like a burden too heavy to bear...
> O LORD, do not forsake me;
> > be not far from me, O my God. (Psalm 38:1–4, 21)

But even when God is disciplining us, he does not emotionally pull away from us or forsake us. As David also writes in Psalm 9:10,

> Those who know your name will trust in you,
> > for you, LORD, have never forsaken those who seek you.

What is the heart of the matter? Wherever you have been, or whatever you have been doing, God will always take you back when you call on him with a humble and contrite heart (Psalm 51:17).

Listen to God serenade you as he repeats the question and then pours forth an answer that only a mother can fully appreciate:

> But Zion said, "The LORD has forsaken me,
> > the Lord has forgotten me."
> "Can a mother forget the baby at her breast
> > and have no compassion on the child she has borne?
> Though she may forget,
> > I will not forget you!" (Isaiah 49:14–15)

God wants us to know that he will never, ever forsake us.

As if that were not enough, the Scripture goes on to say in the next verse, "See, I have engraved you on the palms of my hands" (Isaiah 49:16). This paints a powerful word-picture. The image it conjures up is one of God deeply and permanently etching our names, one by one, onto the soft and strong tissue of his very own hands.

Probably this verse is primarily an allusion to the names of the twelve tribes of Israel that were engraved on stones and fastened to the ephod of the high priest (Exodus 28:9–12), as well as being engraved on the breastpiece worn for making decisions (Exodus 28:15). Whenever the high priest would enter the Holy

Place and meet with God, he would "bear the names of the sons of Israel over his heart on the breastpiece of decision as a continuing memorial before the Lord" (Exodus 28:29).

But perhaps there is also a dramatic foreshadowing here of the ultimate expression of God's love: Jesus' death on the cross and the resulting wounds on his hands that were apparently still evident on his glorified body when he appeared to Thomas after his resurrection (John 20:25–27). And if the wounds on his hands were evident to Thomas on Jesus' glorified body, then one would assume those scars will forever be engraved on the Lord's hands, as a rugged testimony of God's great and wonderful love for us for the rest of eternity!

Just imagine: when Jesus spread out his hands to die on the cross for us, he was sovereignly allowing the Roman soldiers to forever etch onto the palms of his hands the memory of his love for the world. Our name is engraved on the palms of God's hands, forever.

God's Comeback Stories

Some may say, "I know God forgives me, but does he still believe in me after all the times I have failed him? Does he still have vision for me? Does he still have a dream for my life?"

God obviously anticipated this question, and gave us a resounding "Yes!" throughout the pages of Scripture!

Don't you just love a dramatic comeback story? It seems that no one loves a dramatic comeback story more than God himself, since he has authored so many of them. From Gideon and the Midianites, to Jonathan and the Philistines, to David and Goliath—God just loves an underdog!

Have you felt like an underdog lately? Are you feeling like the odds are stacked up against you? Great! The stage is perfectly set for the next big comeback in your life!

Think of all the exciting comeback stories in Scripture. Here are a few examples.

Abraham

Consider the inspiring story of Abraham, the man whom God refused to quit believing in, even after repeated setbacks. Shortly after receiving the promise that God would make him into a great nation through his offspring (Genesis 12:2–3), Abraham proceeds to lie to Pharaoh about Sarah, his wife, calling her his sister so that the Egyptians would not kill him (Genesis 12:10–13). Then Abraham complains to God about remaining childless and taking so long to fulfill his promises regarding the heir that was supposed to come through his family line (Genesis 15:2–3).

How does God feel about Abraham now? Is he still going to believe in him, or is he going to take back his promises and give them to someone else—someone more spiritual and faithful perhaps? Does God still have vision for Abraham, even after he has lied and complained about God's plan?

In Genesis 15:5, God answers our questions in dramatic style as he takes Abraham outside on a clear night to give him an object lesson he would never forget: "'Look up at the heavens and count the stars—if indeed you can count them.' Then he said to him, 'So shall your offspring be.'" To Abraham's credit, he believed God, and this was credited to him as righteousness (Genesis 15:6), and Abraham's legacy was secure as the model of faith (Romans 4:18–25).

It is interesting to note that the final word on Abraham's life was very positive, even though there were chapters in the story that were not. Isn't it comforting to know that the current chapter of your life is not the end of the story, but merely the latest pages to be written? The rest of the story is still up to you!

So if you are not sure that God still believes in you, then walk outside tonight and see the same visual aid of God's promises that the Lord showed Abraham when, in essence, he said, "Look to the sky!" (Genesis 15:5).

Jacob

Then there is the intriguing story of Jacob, the second son of Isaac, who cheated and stole the birthright from his older brother, Esau. When Esau finally catches up with him, Jacob is scared to death that Esau will want to take revenge on him. So, he stays up all night and wrestles in prayer with an angel of God (Genesis 32:22–24).

God is apparently so moved by this desperate display of humble dependence on him in prayer that he grants Jacob favor in Esau's eyes. God even changes Jacob's name from Jacob, which means "deceiver," to Israel, which means "he struggles with God," as a tribute to his willingness to wrestle in prayer and to overcome (Genesis 32:28).

Do you have relationship conflicts? Keep praying, and eventually you too will overcome!

Joseph

A young shepherd boy's dreams came true after God allowed years of suffering to prepare him for the task. It was no secret that Joseph was Jacob's favorite son. His father even made him a richly ornamented robe and gave it to him as a symbol of his special love for him (Genesis 37:3). So, when young Joseph bragged about the dreams that God had given him to rule over his family some day, it is no wonder his brothers took offense at him and were filled with jealousy.

But God made sure that the young man's youthful vanity and pride were sufficiently cleansed from his soul by allowing years of unjust suffering in his life. And after graduating this young student from the divine school of brokenness, God was able to make all of Joseph's dreams come true. God made him the highest ranking official in all the land next to Pharaoh himself, and then used Joseph to rescue his family from famine and financial ruin (Genesis 50:19–21).

Is there unjust suffering in your life? Perhaps it is an essential part of God's plan to make your dreams come true.

Moses

Speaking of God preparing a young man for spiritual service—how about the idealistic young man Moses, who was sure
that God had uniquely prepared him to lead his people out of
Egyptian bondage into the freedom of the Promised Land.
Moses was right about the call, but wrong about the timing.
Apparently God was waiting for forty years in the desert of
refinement before Moses would be inwardly suited to lead God's
people.

In the end, God's word declared Moses to be "a very humble
man, more humble than anyone else on the face of the earth"
(Numbers 12:3). God never gave up on Moses. He was just
waiting for the right timing.

Perhaps you are currently in the desert of refinement. God has
not and will not give up on you. His perfect timing is coming.

Rahab

How about God deciding that the hero of the fall of Jericho
story should be a Canaanite prostitute? Rahab is not only
immortalized in the "hall of faith" of Hebrews 11 for her faithful obedience in hiding the spies (Hebrews 11:31), but she is
also listed as the great, great grandmother of King David, and
the ancestor of Jesus himself (Matthew 1:5). God can overcome
your past, as long as you are willing to be faithful in the present!

Do you feel that your past determines your role? Think of
Rahab and be inspired.

Gideon

Afraid you're not tough enough to play the rugged role that
God has written for you in his adventure screenplay? Consider
the cowardly character of Gideon, who needed no fewer than
seven divine reassurances from God before he had the courage
to rise up and lead God's people against the Midianites (Judges
6:13–39; 7:13–15). God is similarly patient with our own fears,
insecurities and weaknesses.

Samson

Then there is Samson, the rogue judge who was chosen by God to deliver his people, but allowed pride, lust and folly to consume his life. He visited prostitutes (Judges 16:1) and eventually was led like a lamb to the slaughter by the infamous temptress, Delilah (Judges 16:15–21).

But even after totally blowing it, Samson called on the Lord one last time in his weakness and humiliation. He prayed for strength to defeat the Philistines, and God answered that prayer in a dramatic and powerful way, enabling Samson to literally push the huge pillars of the temple aside, crushing more than 3,000 people who were enemies of his God, and killing many more in his death than while he lived (Judges 16:30).

No matter how far we have fallen from grace, God is still able and willing to hear our sincere prayers and use our lives to powerfully glorify his name.

Jehoshaphat

King Jehoshaphat was one of the good kings of Judah. "His heart was devoted to the ways of the LORD" (2 Chronicles 17:6). But he allowed bad company to corrupt his good character (1 Corinthians 15:33) when he aligned himself with the evil King Ahab of the northern kingdom. He even ignored good counsel when the prophet Micaiah warned Jehoshaphat that their political alliance would not succeed (2 Chronicles 18:16–27).

Still, when the fruit of Jehoshaphat's poor decisions ripened, he was wise enough to turn back to God and beg for help, which God gave him, even though the king's predicament was of his own making. Jehoshaphat shows us that we should always turn to God for help, even when we are convicted that our own sins have caused our predicament (2 Chronicles 18:31). God is more merciful than any of us imagines.

Manasseh

In contrast to King Jehoshaphat, King Manasseh was one of

the bad kings of Judah. The Bible says, "He did evil in the eyes of the LORD, following the detestable practices of the nations the LORD had driven out before the Israelites" (2 Chronicles 33:2). Manasseh was actually one of the worst kings of Judah, rebuilding the high places his father, Hezekiah, had demolished and erecting altars to the Baals and making Asherah poles (2 Chronicles 33:3). "He sacrificed his sons in the fire in the Valley of Ben Hinnom, practiced sorcery, divination and witchcraft, and consulted mediums and spiritualists. He did much evil in the eyes of the LORD, provoking him to anger" (2 Chronicles 33:6).

It seems if anyone was a lost cause, it was this guy. But amazingly, the Biblical account goes on to record that after God punished him by sending him into cruel captivity among the Babylonians, Manasseh repents! "In his distress he sought the favor of the LORD his God and humbled himself greatly before the God of his fathers. And when he prayed to him, the LORD was moved by his entreaty and listened to his plea; so he brought him back to Jerusalem and to his kingdom. Then Manasseh knew that the LORD is God" (2 Chronicles 33:12–13).

Manasseh goes on to rebuild the outer walls of Jerusalem, remove all the foreign gods he had formerly set up, and restore the altar of the Lord, sacrificing fellowship and thank offerings on it (2 Chronicles 33:14–16). Listen, if this guy can repent, then there is hope for all of us! God's forgiveness truly knows no bounds.

Job

Physical illness, the loss of a loved one, losing your job or position at work, financial hardships, marital problems, relationship conflicts and just struggling in your relationship with God. Job could relate to all of these challenges—all at the same time!

Talk about disaster striking from out of nowhere! Job never did find out why all of these painful trials came to him. But he did learn how to get through them—by submitting to the mysterious will of the only sovereign God. Job went from resenting his life and questioning God's goodness, to humbling himself before God and trusting that God is in control, even when his life was seemingly spinning out of control (Job 42:1–6).

God wisely gave us this worst-case scenario in the story of Job so that the lessons he learned could easily be applied to our situations as well. How do the lessons of Job apply to your life right now?

The Suffering Woman

Sometimes it is not the dramatic issues that rob our faith, so much as the nagging character flaws, the recurring sins or the long-term illnesses that tend to wear us down over time. The suffering woman in Mark chapter 5 "...had been subject to bleeding for twelve years. She had suffered a great deal under the care of many doctors and had spent all she had, yet instead of getting better, she grew worse" (Mark 5:25).

Do you think she was ever tempted to give up trying? What feelings of defeat and failure did she have to overcome just to dare and try again to be healed? The text reveals her thought process: "When she heard about Jesus, she came up behind him in the crowd and touched his cloak, because she thought, 'If I just touch his clothes, I will be healed.' Immediately her bleeding stopped and she felt in her body that she was freed from her suffering" (Mark 5:27–29).

This time she was healed. But there were no guarantees for her, and there are no guarantees for us. Maybe this is the time you will be healed, and maybe it is not. Maybe you will be healed the next time you cry out, and maybe you won't. There are no guarantees. But one thing is sure: God will help you raise your faith level throughout this trial. "He said to her, 'Daughter, your faith has healed you. Go in peace and be freed from your suffering'" (Mark 5:34). The timing is up to God. But the faith is up to us.

In some cases, God knows it is better not to heal us in the way that we ask for, but to allow the trial to do its refining work in our lives and characters. The apostle Paul confided to the Corinthians that he had "a thorn in his flesh" that he begged the Lord three times to remove, but God told him, "My grace is sufficient for you, for my power is made perfect in weakness" (2 Corinthians 12:9). God may or may not heal us in the ways that we ask him to, but we can be sure that he will always give us the faith and the comfort that we need to make it through. Just remember that it takes long-term faith to make it through long-term trials.

Peter

One of the greatest comeback stories ever told in Scripture is the one about the apostle Peter. He was the original "Rocky Balboa" —knocked down, but not knocked out.

Like the fictional boxing hero, Simon Peter was probably a rough, unsophisticated character. He was a fisherman, not a scholar, an unschooled, ordinary man (Acts 4:13). But Jesus had a special vision for this common man: to be a rock in the faith. And that is basically what Jesus called him, "Rocky," or Peter in the Greek, which means "rock" (John 1:42, see NIV footnote).

But character must be built one challenge at a time. And the gospels reveal that Peter was anything but a rock. He was impulsive, prideful and unstable. And so Peter's story unfolds with many ups and downs: first he is appointed as an apostle (Mark 3:13–16); then he is rebuked for being spiritually dull (Matthew 15:15–16). First he acknowledges that Jesus is the Christ (Matthew 16:16); then he proceeds to rebuke Jesus because he thinks he knows better (Matthew 16:22). First he has the personal devotional time of his life on the Mount of Transfiguration with Jesus (Mark 9:2–8); then later on that day he is rebuked for his lack of faith (Mark 9:19).

Does this sound like a familiar pattern? Maybe that is why Peter's story is so encouraging—he is just like us!

Then comedy becomes tragedy. The hour of Jesus' death is

near, and Jesus tells the apostles,

> "This very night you will all fall away on account of me, for it is written:
>
>> 'I will strike the shepherd,
>> and the sheep of the flock will be scattered.'
>
> But after I have risen, I will go ahead of you into Galilee."
> Peter replied, "Even if all fall away on account of you, I never will."
> "I tell you the truth," Jesus answered, "this very night, before the rooster crows, you will disown me three times."
> But Peter declared, "Even if I have to die with you, I will never disown you." And all the other disciples said the same. (Matthew 26:31–35)

They go to the garden of Gethsemane and pray. Soon, a large crowd armed with swords and clubs come to arrest Jesus. "Then all the disciples deserted him and fled" (Matthew 26:56). But Peter is following the crowd at a distance, wanting to see, but not wanting to be seen (Mark 14:54).

Then it happens.

> A servant girl saw him seated there in the firelight. She looked closely at him and said, "This man was with him."
> But he denied it. "Woman, I don't know him," he said.
> A little later someone else saw him and said, "You also are one of them."
> "Man, I am not!" Peter replied.
> About an hour later another asserted, "Certainly this fellow was with him, for he is a Galilean."
> Peter replied, "Man, I don't know what you're talking about!" Just as he was speaking, the rooster crowed. The Lord turned and looked straight at Peter. Then Peter remembered the word the Lord had spoken to him: "Before the rooster crows today, you will disown me three times." And he went outside and wept bitterly. (Luke 22:56–62)

Can you feel his pain? Perhaps it is your own. Many of us, like

Peter, have started out so faithful and sure of our commitment. Then, like Rocky, we face our opponent, the "Clubber Laings" of our lives—and we fall defeated to the canvas.

There we lie—humiliated and beaten. The entire world is a blur as the referee begins to count us out: "One, two…"

The crowd is so loud, we can't even think. They are jeering and mocking our name. "He's a bum! He's a loser! That guy couldn't even punch his way out of a paper bag!"

"Three, four…" the referee continues. Blood drips from our face, every muscle hurts, and getting back up seems like a monumental task.

But there are other voices in the crowd as well. "You can do it!" shouts one. "Get back up!" shouts another.

"Five, six…" the referee continues.

And then it happens. We hear Jesus calling our name. Not the name the Accuser calls us: "Bum, Loser, Sinner, Imposter." But the name Jesus calls us: "Brother" (Hebrews 2:11), "Friend" (John 15:15) and a special name that will remain a secret just between us (Revelation 2:17). And we get back up before the count reaches "10," ready to fight again, because we have heard the only voice that counts. And we remember our true name.

That is what happened to Peter. Three days after his death, Jesus rose from the dead. And whom do you think he was asking for? The angel tells the three women at the empty tomb,

> "Don't be alarmed," he said, "you are looking for Jesus the Nazarene, who was crucified. He has risen! He is not here. See the place where they laid him. But go, tell his disciples and *Peter*, 'He is going ahead of you into Galilee. There you will see him, just as he told you.'" (Mark 16:6–7, emphasis mine)

Peter is mentioned by name. Soon afterward, Peter is reconciled to Jesus and their friendship is restored (John 21:15–19). And the book of Acts records the great things that Peter went on to do for God. The one who was called "Rocky" by faith, was now a true rock in the faith. His name became his reality.

Your Comeback Story

Do you know who you are?
Do you remember your name?
Or are you blinded by the hurts,
and numbed by the pain?

"You're a loser!"
someone shouts from the crowd.
So you hang your head low,
ashamed and unproud.

But another voice sings
and cheers you on.
It's a voice from the past,
singing your song.

It's the song of your heart,
so precious and pure.
The melody's familiar,
but the words are a blur.

Still the friend continues
calling your name,
and singing the song
with the forgotten refrain.

"Get up! You can do it!"
is the call of the hour.
"We all can be winners,
by God's mighty power!"

—Jeff Chacon

I hope you are encouraged. As we close this chapter, I offer you another poem that uniquely captures the heart of the matter.

The Race

"Quit! Give up! You're beaten!"
they shout at me and plead,
"There's just too much against you now.
This time, you can't succeed."

And as I start to hang my head
in front of failure's face,
my downward fall is broken
by the memory of a race.

And hope refills my weakened will
as I recall that scene.
For just the thought of that short race
rejuvenates my being.

A child's race, not yet young men,
how I remember it well.
Excitement sure, but also fear,
it wasn't hard to tell.

They all lined up so full of hope.
Each thought to win the race,
or tie for first, or if not that,
at least take second place.

And fathers watched from off the side,
each cheering for his son.
And each boy hoped to show his dad
that he would be the one.

The whistle blew, and off they went,
young hearts and hopes afire.
To win, to be the hero there,
was each young boy's desire.

And one boy in particular,
whose dad was in the crowd,
was running in the lead and thought:
"My dad will be so proud."

But as they speeded down the field
across a shallow dip,

the little boy who thought to win,
lost his step and slipped.

Trying hard to catch himself,
his hands threw out a brace.
And amid the laughter of the crowd
he fell flat on his face.

So down he fell and with him hope.
He couldn't win, not now.
Embarrassed, sad, he only wished
to disappear somehow.

But as he fell his dad stood up
and showed his anxious face,
which to the boy so clearly said,
"Get up and win the race."

He quickly rose, no damage done,
behind a bit, that's all,
and ran with all his heart and mind
to make up for his fall.

So anxious to restore himself —
to catch up and to win —
that his mind went faster than his legs
and he slipped and fell again.

He wished that he had quit before
with only one disgrace.
"I'm hopeless as a runner now.
I shouldn't try to race."

But in the laughing crowd he searched
and found his father's face —
that steady look that said again,
"Get up and win the race."

So up he jumped to try again,
ten yards behind the last.
"If I'm going to catch up now,
I better move real fast."

Exerting everything he had

he regained eight or ten.
But trying so hard to regain the lead,
he slipped and fell again.

"Defeat!" He lay there silently.
A tear dropped from his eye.
"There's no sense in running anymore.
Three strikes. I'm out! Why try?"

The will to rise had disappeared.
All hope had fled away.
"So far behind, so error prone —
I'll never go all the way."

"I've lost! So what's the use," he thought.
"I'll live with my disgrace."
But then he thought about his dad
who soon he'd have to face.

"Get up!" an echo whispered in his head.
"Get up and take your place.
You were not meant for failure, son.
Get up and win the race."

"With borrowed will, get up," it said.
"You haven't lost at all.
For winning is no more than this:
to rise each time you fall."

So up he rose to run again
now with a new commit.
He resolved that win or lose this race,
at least he wouldn't quit!

Three times he'd fallen, stumbling.
And three times he rose again.
Now he gave it all he had
and ran as though to win.

They cheered the winning runner
as he crossed the finish line.
Head high, and proud and happy —
he was feeling mighty fine.

But when the fallen youngster
came across the line—last place,
the crowd gave him a bigger cheer—
for finishing the race!

And even though he came in last,
with head bowed low, unproud,
you would have thought he won the race
to hear the cheering crowd!

And to his dad he sadly said,
"I didn't do so well."
"To me you won," his father said.
"You rose each time you fell."

And now when things seem dark and hard
and difficult to face—
the memory of that little boy
helps me in my race.

For all of life is like that race—
with ups and downs and all.
And all you have to do to win
is rise each time you fall.

"Quit! Give up! You're beaten!"
they still shout in my face.
But another voice within me says,
"Get up and win the race!"[1]

—D. H. Groberg

I Dreamed a Dream

There was a time when men were kind,
when their voices were soft,
and their words inviting.
There was a time when love was blind
and the world was a song,
and the song was exciting.

There was a time
then it all went wrong.
I dreamed a dream in times gone by
when hope was high
and life worth living.
I dreamed that love would never die.
I dreamed that God would be forgiving.

Then I was young and unafraid
and dreams were made and used
and wasted.
There was no ransom to be paid,
no song unsung,
no wine untasted.

But the tigers come at night
with their voices soft as thunder
as they tear your hope apart;
as they turn your dream to shame.
He slept a summer by my side
He filled my days with endless wonder.
He took my childhood in his stride—
But he was gone when autumn came.

And still I dream he'll come to me,
that we will live the years together.
But there are dreams that cannot be,
and there are storms we cannot weather.

I had a dream my life would be
so different than this hell I'm living.
So different now from what it seemed.
Now life has killed the dream I dreamed.[1]

Free Homework Pass

Name Nicole Wettach

Date 11·21·05   Period 6

I would like my pass to cover the
homework:

Worksheet 5.3
Practice B

Blake

Alyssa

Johning

Raven

Sisily

2

HIDING IN CAVES

When Dreams Don't Come True

A woman drives by a wedding boutique, and without warning her mind is racing back to her own wedding day—the beautiful gown, the gorgeous flowers, the dreams of forever love and fidelity. And as quickly as it came, the fantasy is gone—aborted by the sad reality of a marriage weighed down with more disappointment than fulfillment, more fear than love, and more questions than answers. And she wonders, *Where do I go from here?*

A man pulls into the church parking lot and steps out of his car on a Wednesday night, trying to gear himself up for yet another midweek service where he will have to face questions about his failures, doubts about his commitment and concerns about his heart. He is not sure when he stopped giving real answers and working hard to guard his own heart, he just knows that something inside has died. And he wonders, *Where do I go from here?*

A young woman is carrying her books to class. She is thinking of nothing in particular until she sees the guys hanging out across campus telling their exaggerated tales of female conquest. And with memories of last night's party still fresh in her mind, she begins to feel hurt and exposed, then mad, and then ashamed. She had said that she wasn't going to cross that line. But she had crossed it anyway. *What went wrong?* she asks herself. And more importantly, *Where do I go from here?*

Cave Dwellers

"Where do I go from here?" Maybe you've asked yourself that same question. Where do we go when our dreams have died? Instead of daring to dream again, the reality is that most of us go into hiding. In the Christian life, there are many different campsites for our souls. Sometimes we find ourselves on the mountaintops of glory. Other times we camp out in the valleys of despair. Still other times we settle in the plateaus of mediocrity. And many times we shrink back into the caves of retreat. The mountaintops are where we go to rejoice. The valleys are where we go to weep. The plateaus are where we go to settle. And the caves are where we go to hide.

Hiding in caves—we've all done it, and we'll probably all do it many times again. Caves are a part of the Christian topography. That is why God includes many stories in his word about cave dwelling; he wants us to learn from them.

Adam and Eve

Adam and Eve were the first to hide in a cave. It happened after they committed the inaugural sin:

> Then the man and his wife heard the sound of the LORD God as he was walking in the garden in the cool of the day, and they hid from the LORD God among the trees of the garden. But the LORD God called to the man, "Where are you?"
>
> He answered, "I heard you in the garden, and I was afraid because I was naked; so I hid." (Genesis 3:8–10)

Adam and Eve's sin led to fear and shame, which led to hiding from God.

Their cave was not a location, but a condition of the heart.

Sin still brings shame and fear today, and God still cries out "Where are you?" When we most pull away is when he draws most near.

Listen to God call out to us in the New Testament when we find ourselves hiding from him in our nakedness:

> Therefore, since we have a great high priest who has gone through the heavens, Jesus the Son of God, let us hold firmly to the faith we profess. For we do not have a high priest who is unable to sympathize with our weaknesses, but we have one who has been tempted in every way, just as we are—yet was without sin. Let us then approach the throne of grace with confidence, so that we may receive mercy and find grace to help us in our time of need. (Hebrews 4:14–16)

Do you see God's hand gently approaching from the outermost region of your self-imposed cave? It's okay. Go ahead and grab hold of it. It's there to guide you out into the light where his grace and mercy await you.

Lot

God called Lot to the mountaintop of glory, but Lot chose instead to hide in the cave of fear. To spare Lot from the destruction of Sodom and Gomorrah, the angels urged Lot and his family, "Flee for your lives! Don't look back, and don't stop anywhere in the plain! Flee to the mountains or you will be swept away!" But this was Lot's response: "No, my lords, please! Your servant has found favor in your eyes, and you have shown great kindness to me in sparing my life. But I can't flee to the mountains; this disaster will overtake me, and I'll die. Look, here is a town near enough to run to, and it is very small. Let me flee to it—it is very small, isn't it? Then my life will be spared" (Genesis 19:17–20).

Soon afterwards, even the small town of Zoar felt unsafe to them and so Lot and his daughters literally moved into a cave (Genesis 19:30).

The key here is Lot's statement to the angel in verse 19, "...I can't flee to the mountains; this disaster will overtake me, and I'll die."

It is never true that we cannot fulfill the plan of God for our lives. No matter how hard Christianity appears to us at the time, no matter how difficult the call of God seems, we must remember that God himself is holding our hand, and that he will keep holding it all the way into heaven…as long as we don't let go. "He will keep you strong to the end, so that you will be blameless on the day of our Lord Jesus Christ. God, who has called you into fellowship with his Son Jesus Christ our Lord, is faithful" (1 Corinthians 1:8–9). "Being confident of this, that he who began a good work in you will carry it on to completion until the day of Christ Jesus" (Philippians 1:6). "The one who calls you is faithful and he will do it" (1 Thessalonians 5:24).

Don't give up on yourself, because God never gives up on you!

Moses

The desert was Moses' cave. At first he was hiding from Pharaoh, but soon he was hiding from God. Near the end of the account of God's call to Moses, we hear the unmistakable voice of a cave dweller as Moses pleads: "O Lord, please send someone else to do it" (Exodus 4:13).

Sound familiar? God had intended the desert to humble Moses. But the fact is, it almost killed him by destroying both his selfish and his godly ambition. Don't let the caves kill your dreams. Don't let your failures be fatal. Remember that God "disciplines those he loves" (Hebrews 12:6), his grace is sufficient for you (2 Corinthians 12:9), and "no temptation has seized you except what is common to man. And God is faithful; he will not let you be tempted beyond what you can bear. But when you are tempted, he will also provide a way out so that you can stand up under it" (1 Corinthians 10:13).

A good friend of mine, one of my all-time favorite comeback preachers, likes to say, "Every moment in my life has prepared me for this moment. And this moment is preparing me for the next." That was certainly true for Moses. And it is just as true for each one of us today.

Gideon

Gideon was also hiding in a cave when God called him to

spiritual service. He was threshing wheat in a winepress so he could hide from the Midianites (Judges 6:1–3, 11). The angel's greeting made Gideon wonder who he was talking to: "The LORD is with you, mighty warrior" (Judges 6:12). Apparently the Lord saw Gideon very differently than Gideon saw himself: "How can I save Israel? My clan is the weakest in Manasseh, and I am the least in my family" (Judges 6:15).

Does that sound like your situation? Do you feel like the weakest member of the weakest group in your church? That is not how God sees you. God sees you as a "mighty warrior" who walks with a mighty God!

God eventually used Gideon to lead the woefully outnumbered Israelites to victory over the powerful Midianites. The one who was hiding in a winepress indeed became "a mighty warrior" for God, and so can we. Remember that God plus one always makes a majority!

Elijah

What about the mighty prophet Elijah? Surely we would never find him running away and hiding from anyone. I mean, this is one of the most courageous prophets of all time! Elijah is the one who raised a widow's son from the dead (1 Kings 17:7–24) and then single-handedly took on 450 false prophets of Baal and 400 prophets of Asherah in the dramatic spiritual showdown on top of Mount Carmel (1 Kings 18:16–40). In fact, Elijah walked so closely with God, that he didn't even die a natural death, but instead was simply taken up in a whirlwind to heaven by blazing horses and chariots of fire (2 Kings 2:11). (Now that's a prayer walk!) And the New Testament records that during one of Jesus' most memorable prayers it was Elijah and Moses that appeared to him on the Mount of Transfiguration (Luke 9:30–31). So Elijah was a spiritual hero!

And yet, the Bible records that right after the monumental victory of Mount Carmel, "Elijah was afraid and ran for his life.... He came to a broom tree, sat down under it and prayed that he might die. 'I have had enough, LORD' he said. 'Take my life; I am no better than my ancestors.' ...There he went into a *cave* and spent the night" (1 Kings 19:3–4, 9 emphasis added).

Here we find the venerable prophet Elijah afraid, discouraged and wanting to quit. Why? What would cause such an incredible man of God to sink to these spiritual depths?

The answer is both sobering and encouraging—sobering in that we are all vulnerable to discouragement, Satan's mighty and powerful weapon; but encouraging in that Elijah sank to these emotional depths and then rose again, so then maybe there is hope for us all.

Simply put, Elijah felt like a failure because the one person he was most trying to help spiritually with the awesome display of God's mighty power on Mount Carmel was the king himself, King Ahab (1 Kings 18:16–19). But right when it looked like the king might come around to worshiping the true God again (and thus triumphantly restoring spiritual leadership to the Israelites), his wife, the evil Queen Jezebel, poisoned his mind and turned him back to false idol worship (1 Kings 21:25–26). She then sent a message to the prophet Elijah, threatening his life. This pushed him over the edge and into the emotional tailspin that became his real and imagined cave (1 Kings 19:2–9).

Can you relate? Have you ever tried to help someone spiritually, only to see them plunge themselves into sin and spiritual ruin anyway? If you are a disciple of Jesus, then I know that you can relate. People-helpers will always suffer the deep emotional pain of watching those we love fall into sin and perhaps even walk away from God. It is a participation in the very heart of God, who feels more pain over the fallen than any of us can possibly imagine (Genesis 6:5–6; Matthew 23:37–38; Romans 9:1–4).

But we must not allow Satan's weapons of discouragement, hurt and perceived failure to push us into the cave of retreat for very long. If we stay in that cave too long, we will eventually die.

And many more who are already spiritually dead will never have a chance to live.

I know. I've been there.

I'll never forget the young couple that my wife and I had the privilege of sharing the gospel with in Denver several years ago. They became Christians and gave their lives willingly to Jesus Christ, causing great celebration in their hearts, ours and the angels in heaven (Luke 15:10).

But the rejoicing was short-lived. Soon after their sincere conversion, a mutual friend of ours poisoned their minds with lies about the church, their new faith and us. By the time we found out what had happened, the young couple that had once been so happy about their newfound faith in God through Jesus Christ had become cold, disillusioned and embittered. In spite of our best efforts, they refused to come back to the faith, asking us to please stay away from them and not try to change their minds. We sadly honored that decision, telling them that if they ever wanted to come back to God that we were sure he would gladly receive them back with open arms, rejoicing as the father does in the parable of the prodigal son (Luke 15:11–24).

Unfortunately, they never returned.

And neither did our grieving hearts; not for a while anyway.

We were wounded; deeply hurt both by the pain of seeing two souls leaving the best thing in their lives (Hebrews 6:4–6), and by the betrayal of the friend who had turned them from the faith. We were discouraged in our own faith, wondering if it was even worth it to try and save lost souls if this is what would happen to them eventually. We were still faithful Christians ourselves, but the light had faded from our eyes, and the bounce had disappeared from our steps. We had given away our hearts, and our hearts had been stepped on. Was it worth it to give away our hearts again? It certainly did not feel like it at the time.

But God healed our hearts. The passage of time, the regular reading of God's word, and the fellowship of other friends revived our spirits. Soon we were back on track, giving our hearts away again as God commands us.

We learned some valuable lessons. We learned that persecution and things that cause people to stumble are bound to come (Matthew 5:11–12, 2 Timothy 3:12, 1 Peter 4:12–19), but we must nurture our own hearts through these times so that our spiritual roots will be deep and we will stay faithful through the discouragement (Mark 4:17).

We learned that feeling the pain of seeing those you love make mistakes is participating in the sufferings of Christ himself and helps us to know him and to have fellowship with him in a deeper and more profound way (Philippians 3:10–11, Colossians 1:24).

We also learned that crying for ourselves is okay for a night, but not for a lifetime. The next time a similar event happened to me, I decided I would cry just once for myself, and from then on cry only for the person who had left God (which I did many times). Pity is one of the godly sons of compassion. But self-pity is one of the ungodly sons of selfishness.

Elijah was swimming in self-pity when the Lord appeared to him in the form of a great and powerful wind, an earthquake, a fire and finally a gentle whisper: "What are you doing here, Elijah?" (1 Kings 19:13). Elijah said he felt like he was the only one left doing God's will (Kings 19:14). But God assured him that there were many more good-hearted people that were still faithful to him and had not fallen away (1 Kings 19:18).

Sometimes it seems that there are more defeats than victories in the Christian life. But God assures us that the book has already been written, and he definitely wins in the end (Revelation 21–22). You're on the right team. Don't quit now!

Finally, God directs Elijah to gather three partners to help him out: Hazael, Jehu and Elisha (1 Kings 19:15–17). I have found that having a few close partners in the work of the Lord has helped my wife and me more than anything else to stay encouraged through the difficult times in life. The old saying is true: "Friendship doubles our joys and divides our sorrows."

Who are your partners in the Lord? Do they know you inside and out? Are they a real help to you in times of trouble? Are you a help to them? Coming out of the caves is much easier when you have a circle of friends to embrace you. Seek them out as Elijah did, and like that great prophet of God, you too can have a great spiritual comeback!

John the Baptist

Can you imagine seeing what John the Baptist saw? He literally saw heaven open and the Spirit of God descending like a dove on Jesus at his baptism (Matthew 3:16). Wow, that must have been quite a sight!

Can you imagine hearing what John the Baptist heard? He heard a voice from heaven speaking to Jesus and saying, "This is my Son, whom I love; with him I am well pleased" (Matthew 3:17). I'll bet he never forgot that voice!

Can you imagine knowing what John the Baptist knew? It was John who first announced Jesus' identity as the savior of the world in John 1:29: "The next day John saw Jesus coming toward him and said, 'Look, the Lamb of God, who takes away the sin of the world!'"

I'll bet John the Baptist never struggled with his faith in Jesus...

But actually, that is exactly what happened.

"When John heard in prison what Christ was doing, he sent his disciples to ask him, 'Are you the one who was to come, or should we expect someone else?'" (Matthew 11:2–3).

Amazing! John the Baptist is wondering if Jesus is the one. The very one who had first announced Jesus' identity, now doubts it! The very hands that baptized Jesus, are now being thrown up into the air in doubt and uncertainty. And the very lips that testified of Jesus, "...this is the Son of God" (John 1:34), are now asking, "Are you the one who was to come, or should we expect someone else?"

How can that be? How does such a spiritually strong man of God get so weak in his faith?

The answer is found in the first part of Matthew 11: "When John heard *in prison...*" (emphasis added).

You see, John the Baptist had been thrown into prison by King Herod because John was publicly denouncing the king's immoral lifestyle (Mark 6:17–20). After some time in prison, John probably got discouraged, disillusioned and started to doubt. "Where is God in all of this? How come I have to suffer in solitude while Herod does evil and seems to get away with it? And why isn't Jesus doing anything about it? If he really is the promised Messiah of Scripture, why isn't he bringing about justice to this obviously unjust situation?"

John's dreams of the kingdom of God had been shattered. His faith was low and he was struggling.

John's prison had bars holding him captive. But perhaps the real prison that held him now was the prison of his soul, held captive by the bars of doubt and discouragement. This is the cave in which John the Baptist found himself.

It reminds me of the popular song "Torn," by Natalie Imbruglia. This song rips my heart out every time I hear it:

> I'm all out of faith;
> this is how I feel.
> I'm cold and I'm ashamed,
> lying naked on the floor.
> Illusion never changed
> into something real.
> I'm wide awake and
> I can see the perfect sky is torn.
> You're a little late.
> I'm already torn.[2]

Like the songwriter, John is torn. He is hurt. And he is at a crossroads in his faith, struggling just to hang on.

Of course the real power of this story is not in John's question, but in Jesus' answer.

How will Jesus respond? Will he get mad at John for daring to doubt his identity? Will he be indignant with John for struggling spiritually after all that God has done for him? Will Jesus tell John's disciples to go back and rebuke him for his faithlessness?

"Jesus replied, 'Go back and report to John what you hear and see: The blind receive sight, the lame walk, those who have leprosy are cured, the deaf hear, the dead are raised, and the good news is preached to the poor. Blessed is the man who does not fall away on account of me.... I tell you the truth: Among those born of women there has not risen anyone greater than John the Baptist'" (Matthew 11:4–6, 11).

Jesus doesn't rebuke John for struggling. Instead he proceeds to encourage him and pour faith into him! Jesus points to the miraculously changed lives all around him and gives John fresh reason to believe. "Look at the miracles," Jesus seems to say. "I am fulfilling the Old Testament prophecies about the Messiah. And by the way, I still believe in you, John. Don't fall away."

Wow, Jesus is so encouraging! He still believes in John, even when John is struggling to believe in Jesus. And that is how Jesus feels about you and me. He still believes in us, even when we are struggling to believe in him.

Are you hurting? Have prayers that seemed to go unanswered damaged your faith? Can you relate to John the Baptist in his hour of doubt and disillusionment?

Then know that our Lord is gentle. "A bruised reed he will not break, and a smoldering wick he will not snuff out" (Matthew 12:20). And let him fill *your* heart with fresh faith as he points to all the miracles around *you* and reminds you where they come from. "Don't be deceived, my dear brothers. Every good and perfect gift is from above, coming down from the

Father of the heavenly lights, who does not change like shifting shadows" (James 1:16–17).

Even when we doubt God, he never doubts us.

Everybody Hurts Sometimes

The truth is that we all struggle in our faith at different times in our lives. We struggle to submit our wills to God's, and we find ourselves running *from* him instead of *to* him more often than we would like to admit. As long as we are sinners, we are going to continue to struggle with sin and the consequences of shame and fear that accompany it.

But God is very patient with our weaknesses, eager to help us through our difficult times, and always coaxing us out of our caves and back onto the narrow road.

One time I was feeling a bit down and heard this almost hypnotic song on the radio that seemed to be sent from God to soothe my soul. It is called "Everybody Hurts Sometimes" and is by REM. The comforting sound of the music is complemented by equally comforting words. I hope they help to heal your heart:

> *When you've had enough, hang on.*
> *Don't let yourself go,*
> *cuz everybody cries,*
> *and everybody hurts—sometimes.*
>
> *Sometimes everything is wrong.*
> *And you feel like letting go;*
> *you think you've had too much—*
> *hold on.*
>
> *Cuz everybody hurts*
> *sometimes..."*[3]

David

If anyone ever knew about hurting, it was David, the psalmist and king. David literally hid in caves. He was hiding from King Saul, who was trying to take his life. "David left Gath and escaped to the *cave* of Adullam" (1 Samuel 22:1, emphasis added). David was hiding from unrighteous leadership in the kingdom of God. He was not in the caves by choice, but by necessity. David was not hiding *from* God, but *in* God. "Rescue me from my enemies, O Lord, for *I hide myself in you*" (Psalm 143:9, emphasis added).

This is a different type of hiding than the other examples listed earlier; it is hiding in God, which is the best thing we can do in difficult situations.

If you find yourself in similar circumstances, then read carefully Psalm 57, and let it teach you how to hide yourself in God. Unjust suffering was at the very heart of the cross of Jesus Christ, and it is at the very heart of our crosses as well (1 Peter 2:21). There is no mistake. God is not unaware of your circumstances. You are on the right road—the road to Calvary.

Resist the urge to fight back. Remember the example of Jesus: "When they hurled their insults at him, he did not retaliate; when he suffered, he made no threats. Instead he entrusted himself to him who judges justly" (1 Peter 2:23). That last sentence is what hiding yourself in God is all about: entrusting yourself to him who judges justly.

I love the lines from Psalm 25 that we often sing in worship:

Unto thee, O Lord,
do I lift up my soul.
O my God, I trust in thee.
Oh, let me not be ashamed,
let not my enemies triumph over me.

I have lifted up my soul to God many times in my Christian life with these words. And I can tell you that God has always answered my prayers to not be ashamed and not let my enemies triumph over me. Short time or long, in the end God will prove himself faithful. Don't run from him and hide in caves of your own making. Instead, hide yourself in him.

Listen. The Lord is singing you a song, when you least expect it, and most need it...

What If I Were To Tell You

What if I were to tell you
  that I love you more than ever?
What if I were to tell you
  that you mean that much to me?

What if I were to tell you
  that I'm proud of all you've done?
What if I were to tell you
  that I'm proud of who you've become?

What if I were to tell you
  that the trials are not a mistake?
What if I were to tell you
  that I wish I could take your place?

What if I were to tell you
  that I know what you're going through?
What if I were to tell you
  that I long to show myself to you?

I love you, my darling,
  more than you'll ever realize.
I love you, my sweetheart,
  as my eyes begin to cry.

One day I'll show you
  things you're not permitted to see.
One day you'll see me,
  and the truth will set you free!

What if I were to tell you
  that I know what you're going through?
What if I were to tell you
  that I long to show myself to you?

—Jeff Chacon

3

WHAT IF I WERE TO TELL YOU

God Still Loves You

Do you hear God singing to you?

God loves music. Music was his idea. And the Bible says "...he will rejoice over you with singing" (Zephaniah 3:17). Can you imagine? What must God's voice sound like? One day we will hear it with our own ears in heaven. But even now we can hear it with our hearts if we will just learn to listen (Matthew 13:15).

God sings to us in the breathtaking beauty of a clear blue sky on a cool winter's day. He croons and caresses us with his warm arms on a hot summer's day, and showers us with tears of compassion on gray and cloudy days. He is always singing to us! He sings through nature, he sings through people, he sings through his word, and if you will quiet your soul long enough to hear him, I am sure you'll hear him singing through his Spirit inside of you.

God loves to sing to us! And yet, so many times we don't here his voice. Why is that? There are many reasons, such as not reading his word, not praying, not being spiritually minded, and not listening to others.

But there is another huge reason that many times we cannot hear the voice of God—one that many of us fail to even recognize.

It is because there is another voice vying for our attention. It is not the voice of God, nor is it our own voice. It is the voice of another—luring, persuading, lying and condemning.

The Accuser

He's your worst nightmare.
He's more cunning than a serial killer,
more dangerous than a terrorist,
and more powerful than all the armies of the world combined.
He's sneaky, underhanded and covert.
He is the demise of many a good man, woman and nation.
He is very good at what he does.
In fact, he's the best.
He's a killer, a liar and a thief.
But most people never even know that they've been taken by him.
You have...
He's stolen your purity,
damaged your relationships,
and crippled your walk with God.
He's been in your house,
in your car,
in your bedroom,
and in your heart.
He fights dirty,
hits below the belt,
and doesn't play by the rules.
He has one goal in life:
to destroy you and everything that you love and hold dear.
And he won't stop
until he sees you burn in hell—
for eternity.
What is his name?
He is called Lucifer or Beelzebub,
the ruler of darkness,
the prince of this world.
He is called Belial, Abaddon and Apollyn.
He is called "the god of this age."
He is our accuser, our adversary, and our enemy.

He is referred to as "the serpent,"
"the tempter"
and "the evil one."
He is "the angel of the abyss,"
"the prince of demons,"
"the ruler of the kingdom of the air…"
He is the devil.
And his name is Satan.

—Jeff Chacon

Most people make jokes about him. But he is no joking matter. Satan is mentioned more than a hundred times in Scripture. Jesus himself mentions him eighteen times in the Gospels.

The New Testament writers warn us to be alert and to resist him (1 Peter 5:9), to be aware of his schemes so that we are not outwitted by him (2 Corinthians 2:11), and to put on the full armor of God so that we can take our stand against him (Ephesians 6:11). He is a roaring lion, looking for someone to devour (1 Peter 5:8). And though his schemes are many, they generally fall into two main categories: deception and accusation.

First, he deceives us into thinking it is no big deal to sin this one little time. After all, God is not looking, or perhaps he does not want us to know how delicious sin really tastes (Genesis 3:1–5).

Of course, this is a lie, because Satan is a liar. Jesus said of him, "When he lies, he speaks his native language, for he is a liar and the father of lies" (John 8:44).

But then, once we give in to the temptation and sin, he reverses his strategy and becomes an accuser (Revelation 12:10). "I can't believe you did that! Your sin just shows what an evil person you really are! Who are you trying to fool, acting like a Christian? You are a hypocrite and a fake! God will not forgive you this time. You've gone too far. Just give up and give in to your desires. Your heart is evil anyway. Who could love someone like you?"

Sound familiar? Of course it does. He has been shooting these same flaming arrows at all mankind for thousands of years now (1 Corinthians 10:13, Ephesians 6:16). And why change his strategy? It works pretty well, doesn't it?

Of course these accusations are also lies. But here is the catch: we actually believe them. We already feel horrible about all the sins that we commit against God, and the evil thoughts that run through our minds sometimes. "So, how can God love a person like me," we reason, "when I have such a wicked and evil heart? It makes more sense that he would give up on me and give his love to someone else, someone better than me."

But God says, "Can a mother forget the baby at her breast and have no compassion on the child she has borne? Though she may forget, I will not forget you!" (Isaiah 49:15).

If you have children, then you understand this concept. And even if you don't, you still can imagine it. Would you stop loving your children because of their poor behavior?

And if we love our own children through thick and thin, how much more does our heavenly father love us? (Matthew 7:11).

Clothed with Christ

One of my favorite passages in the Bible is found in Zechariah 3. It is a very descriptive scene of what goes on in the spiritual realm between God, Satan and our hearts: "Then he showed me Joshua the high priest standing before the angel of the LORD, and Satan standing at his right side to accuse him" (Zechariah 3:1). Joshua symbolizes us, standing before the angel of the LORD, who represents God. Meanwhile, Satan stands beside us, hissing and hurling his hateful accusations against us to God, our judge. The footnote in the NIV Bible for this verse even reminds us that the name "Satan" means "accuser."

So, what will happen next? Satan's accusations are hateful, but true. We are guilty of all of the sins Satan accuses us of— and more! We have disobeyed God and fallen short of his glory again and again (Romans 3:23). He is right! We stand accused before the sovereign judge of the universe, and we are guilty—guilty as charged!

But the angel of the Lord's response is as surprising to us as it is to Satan himself: "The LORD rebuke you, Satan! The LORD, who has chosen Jerusalem, rebuke you! Is not this man a burning stick snatched from the fire?" (Zechariah 3:2).

The Lord rebukes Satan, not us! God is indignant at Satan, not because he is lying about our sins, but because he is lying about our forgiveness! Yes, we are burning sticks, but we have been snatched from the fire by God himself. Then the angel of the Lord does an even more incredible thing:

> Now Joshua was dressed in filthy clothes as he stood before the angel. The angel said to those who were standing before him, "Take off his filthy clothes."
> Then he said to Joshua, "See, I have taken away your sin, and I will put rich garments on you."
> Then I said, "Put a clean turban on his head." So they put a clean turban on his head and clothed him, while the angel of the LORD stood by. (Zechariah 3:3–5)

Joshua's filthy clothes represent the filthy sins that clothe each of our hearts. The Lord takes our filthy clothes off, washes our hearts clean, and then puts new clothes on us. This is the essence of what it means to be clothed with Christ: "You are all sons of God through faith in Christ Jesus, for all of you who were baptized into Christ have clothed yourselves with Christ" (Galatians 3:26–27).

If we have been baptized into Christ, then we have been clothed with the righteousness of Christ. When God looks down on us from heaven, he does not see the filthy rags of our sins anymore, but the pure robes of Jesus Christ adorning our hearts.

That is what it means to be clothed with Christ. "Therefore, there is now *no condemnation* for those who are in Christ Jesus" (Romans 8:1, emphasis added).

Now, that is great news!

Even though you know that God loves and forgives you, have you ever felt like God doesn't like you or doesn't want to be around you?

Sure you have. We all have. It is because sometimes we don't like ourselves and don't want to be around ourselves, so we reason that no one else would either. Of course, nothing could be further from the truth. God is madly in love with us and wants nothing more than to be with us. So, why do we think that way? Many of us don't *feel* the love of God as we should because we don't *know* the love of God as we should.

The Singer

Moses wanted to know God better.

God had called Moses to lead the people out of Egypt, through the Red Sea and into the desert. And now God was chiseling out two stone tablets to give Moses in order to teach the people his laws (Exodus 34).

But Moses wanted to know the author of the laws. He wanted to know who this God was who was speaking to him from behind the dark cloak of secrecy on Mount Sinai. And so, he asked God, "Now show me your glory" (Exodus 33:18).

> And the LORD said, "I will cause all my goodness to pass in front of you, and I will proclaim my name, the LORD, in your presence. I will have mercy on whom I will have mercy, and I will have compassion on whom I will have compassion. But," he said, "you cannot see my face, for no one may see me and live."
> Then the LORD said, "There is a place near me where you may stand on a rock. When my glory passes by, I will put you in a cleft in the rock and cover you with my hand until I have passed by. Then I will remove my hand and you will see my back; but my face must not be seen." (Exodus 33:19–23)

Can you imagine the anticipation? God says, "I will cause all my goodness to pass in front of you…" Wow! What does "goodness" look like? Does it have a color, an aura or a shape? Does it glow? Does it pulsate and throb with feeling and emotion?

And what will God say about himself? Many have endeavored to describe God, but how will God describe himself? What qualities of his character will he choose to emphasize? What is the Lord's true name, anyway?

Imagine the excitement if you were Moses: God's going to put me in the cleft of a rock, cover me with his hand so I can't see his face, and then show me his back, while he proclaims his true name to me—would you be able to sleep the night before that date?

The next morning finally arrived, and Moses made his way back up to Mount Sinai to meet with God. Here is the Biblical account of what happened:

> Then the LORD came down in the cloud and stood there with him and proclaimed his name, the LORD. And he passed in front of Moses, proclaiming, "The LORD, the LORD, the compassionate and gracious God, slow to anger, abounding in love and faithfulness, maintaining love to thousands, and forgiving wickedness, rebellion and sin. Yet he does not leave the guilty unpunished; he punishes the children and their children for the sin of the fathers to the third and fourth generation."
> Moses bowed to the ground at once and worshiped.
> (Exodus 34:5–8)

I think all of us would have bowed down to the ground and worshiped too!

But the amazing thing is that the indescribable God described himself in two sentences to Moses. Not surprisingly, only slight variations of these same two sentences became the most often repeated description of God in all the Scriptures, found also in Numbers 14:18, Nehemiah 9:17, Psalm 86:15, Psalm 103:8, Psalm 145:8–9, Jeremiah 32:18, Joel 2:13 and Jonah 4:2.

It is simply who God is, according to God himself.

Who is God? What are the words and phrases he uses to

describe himself?

- Compassionate
- Gracious
- Slow to anger
- Abounding in love and faithfulness
- Maintaining love to thousands
- Forgiving wickedness, rebellion and sin
- Yet not leaving the guilty unpunished

Is that your view of God? If not, then you have a wrong concept of God. The verses do not need to change; your opinion of him needs to change. This is the God of the Bible. This is the God who is deeply in love with you. This is the singer who delights to quiet you with his love and rejoice over you with singing.

The Song

I'll take care of you.

> A father to the fatherless, a defender of widows,
>   is God in his holy dwelling.
> God sets the lonely in families,
>   he leads forth the prisoners with singing....
> (Psalm 68:5–6)

Don't you just love this verse? It comforts us with compassion, heals us with hope, and strengthens us with...singing! Yes, here is another verse that talks about how God sings to us!

And what is he singing? "Come to me, you who are fatherless, and let me be your spiritual father. Take heart, you who are widowed and let me defend your cause. Cheer up, you who are lonely, and let me give you a spiritual family. Follow me, you who are imprisoned by your fears, your past or your circumstances, and let me encourage you with my song! It's all right; I'll take care of you."

I'm eager to bless you.

> "Which of you, if his son asks for bread, will give him a stone? Or if he asks for a fish, will give him a snake? If you, then, though you are evil, know how to give good gifts to your children, how much more will your Father in heaven give good gifts to those who ask him!" (Matthew 7:9–11)

Jesus paints a picture of God, sitting on the edge of his seat, eager to bless us. We sometimes imagine God to be stingy with his blessings, like Scrooge in *A Christmas Carol*.

But nothing could be further from the truth! God loves to lavish his grace on us (Ephesians 1:7–8) and has more in his storeroom of blessings than we can possibly imagine! He is just dying to "throw open the floodgates of heaven and pour out so much blessing that you [we] will not have enough room for it" (Malachi 3:10).

So, as Jesus urges us, go ahead and pray to the one who wants to bless you (Matthew 7:9-11).

Never doubt that I am with you and for you.

> "Never will I leave you; never will I forsake you." (Hebrews 13:5)

Man's love is conditional. It can be diminished or taken away, and so we constantly feel like we have to earn it, like grades on a report card.

But God's love is not like man's love. God's love is unconditional (1 John 4:10).

God says: "Never will I leave you; never will I forsake you" (Hebrews 13:5).

We say: "But what about when I'm blowing it, and I'm struggling with sin?"

God says: "Never will I leave you...."

We say: "But what about when I'm struggling with my faith and giving in to doubt, fear and resentment?"

God says: "Never will I forsake you...."

Does God condone our sin? No. He calls us to repent every time (Hebrews 10:26–31). But we "*stand* in grace" (Romans 5:2, emphasis added), and "we *have* redemption, the forgiveness of sins" (Colossians 1:14, emphasis added). We don't move in and out of God's favor depending on our latest good or bad deed, since our deeds are not the basis of God's love for us (Ephesians 2:8–9).

Man's love is conditional. But God's love is unconditional. Never doubt that God is with you and for you.

You are the love of my life.

> As a bridegroom rejoices over his bride,
> so will your God rejoice over you. (Isaiah 62:5)

I remember watching her walk up the aisle, wearing white, gliding gracefully toward me, and with a look of love in her eyes. Watching a bride walk up the aisle is one of the most beautiful sights you will ever see, especially if you are the bridegroom. Is it possible that God views us that way?

Read the verse above again. Now believe it.

We are Cinderella, and the Lord is Prince Charming. We need to live with a sense of wonder, feel that glass slipper fit, and know that though we are dressed in rags, we were born for royalty.[1]

Even though I have to discipline you, I still love you.

> My son, do not despise the LORD's discipline
> and do not resent his rebuke,
> because the LORD disciplines those he loves,
> as a father the son he delights in. (Proverbs 3:11–12)

I had to learn from the Bible that discipline is a part of love because growing up, I was raised with very little discipline from my parents, and yet I knew that my parents loved me. So, how could discipline be a part of love? I've learned that though my parents did the best job they could, they also made mistakes (as all of us parents do). But God does not make mistakes. He is the perfect parent. And he tells us that his discipline is evidence of his love.

God does not set aside his love in order to discipline us. He leans forward in his love and disciplines us as needed because his love moves him to do it. "God disciplines us for our good" (Hebrews 12:10). He is treating us as his dearly loved children when he disciplines us. Don't resent it. Be grateful for it and learn from it because it comes from a heart of love.

I forgive you—let's start over.

> "Their sins and lawless acts I will remember no more."
> (Hebrews 10:17)

Don't you just love that about God? He's so eager to forgive and forget.

Sometimes we confess the same sins over and over to God even after we have sincerely repented and asked for forgiveness for them. And God doesn't know what we're talking about—because he had already forgiven us the first time.

Love "keeps no record of wrongs" (1 Corinthians 13:5), and "God is love" (1 John 4:16), therefore God has a short memory about our sins. He is just as eager to move on from them as we are—probably more so. Do you ever wish you could just start all over again and be rebaptized? There is no need to be rebaptized. Just sincerely confess and renounce your sins, and your soul is as spotless and clean as the day you were first baptized (Proverbs 28:13; 1 John 1:5–7).

That is because God is always willing to forgive and start over.

I'd rather die than live without you.

> "For God so loved the world that he gave his one and only Son, that whoever believes in him shall not perish but have eternal life." (John 3:16)

When you think about who is saying this, it gives the statement even more weight. Jesus and the Father are one (John 17:22). So, in essence, God through Jesus is saying, "Let me tell you how much I love you: I'd rather die than live without you."

Now of course Jesus' death was temporary "because it was impossible for death to keep its hold on him" (Acts 2:24). But he died for us nonetheless. And that death serves as eternal proof of the magnitude of God's love for us (1 John 4:9). Make no mistake about it: he would rather die a temporary death on earth, than live an eternity without you.

I love you.

> "Since you are precious and honored in my sight,
> and because I love you..." (Isaiah 43:4)

There is just something about those words: I love you.

I want to hear him say, "Well done" (Matthew 25:21). I want to hear him say, "Great job! I'm proud of you" (1 Corinthians 4:5). I want to hear him say, "You made it! Here's your crown" (James 1:12). I want to hear God say a lot of things to me some day. But more than anything else, I want God one day to look me straight in the eye and say, "I love you." Until that day, there is Isaiah 43:4. Read it again and let it sink in. Read it every day, several times a day, if you want to. Just do not ever forget it.

God loves you.

For those tears I died.

It was the first song I ever learned at church in which the lyrics portrayed Jesus as actually singing to us. Most songs of praise are from us to God. But this one is from God to us.

I was young and single in the Lord when I first learned it, and felt alone in my trials, except for God. He was there for me when I needed him most. And I will always love him for that. See if you can relate to the first verse, and then let Jesus soothe your soul in the refrain. It is called "For Those Tears I Died":

You said you'd come and share all my sorrows.
You said you'd be there for all my tomorrows.

I came so close to sending you away,
but just like you promised,
you came here to stay.
I just had to pray.

And Jesus said: "Come to the water, stand by my side.
I know you are thirsty, you won't be denied.

I felt every tear drop when in darkness you cried.
And I strove to remind you that for those tears I died."[2]

Do you hear God singing to you? He is singing, "What if I were to tell you that I still love you?"

Dare to dream again.

It's All About Love

They run after pleasure
    and we call it sin.
We run after favor
    and never get in.

And the prophets howl,
    while the wise man cries:
"It's all about love,
    and the rest is all lies."

"Stop trusting in your good,"
    God says to us all.
"The best of them tried,
    and hit the same wall.

"Give me your hand.
    Then give me your heart.
We'll head for the sky,
    and that's just the start!

"Shut your eyes tight;
    don't look (if you dare)—
Then jump in my arms
    and swim in my care.

"What do I want?
    Do you really have to ask?
What can man do?
    What performance, what task?

"I want what's of value
    but just can't be bought.
I want the one thing
    even God's not got.

"I want you to want me
    more than life itself;
more than food or pleasure
    or even your health.

"I want you to think of me
    morning, noon and night.
And I want you to call
    and I want you to write.

"I've always wanted you!
    Oh why can't you see?
And now I want you
    to always want me."

And the prophets howl,
    while the wise man cries:
"It's all about love,
    and the rest is all lies."

                                        —*Jeff Chacon*

4

IT'S ALL ABOUT LOVE

Our Purpose Is to Be with God

What is our purpose in life? Why were we created? What was God's intention in creating us? If you have children of your own, then you know. And even if you don't have children, then you probably still know.

My wife used to joke that her parents didn't have children; they had slaves! She was sure that the purpose for which they were born was so that her parents could have someone to do the chores around the house. Of course, we laugh about that kind of thinking now, but as kids many of us thought that way, and it caused us to have hurt feelings toward our parents.

Many of us as Christians have done the same thing. We confuse our task with our purpose, and it ends up hurting our relationship with God. We feel more like his slaves than his children.

Imagine for a moment that you are tucking one of your little children into bed at night. You have read him his favorite bedtime story, heard all about his day, and are now getting ready to kiss him goodnight. With a tender look of love in your eyes you softly whisper to him, "I love you, Son." And he looks back at you with his sweet little face and says, "Of course you do; I did all my chores today."

A little taken aback by this unexpected response, you pause

for a moment to collect your thoughts, and then earnestly reply, "Well, I'm glad you did your chores today, Son, but that's not why I love you. I love you because you're my son."

Seeming to totally understand and yet obviously missing the point, your son quickly responds, "Yes, and I remember what you said about how important it is to help out around the house and get my jobs done before I play, and I did that today; so that's why you love me."

More concerned than before, and even feeling a little agitated at this potentially significant misunderstanding, you swallow hard and then proceed to explain: "I want you to do your chores around the house, Son. We all need to do our part to keep this house clean, and I'm happy that you did your part today. But that's not why I love you. I loved you long before you were able to do chores around the house, and I'll love you long after you've stopped doing chores in this house. I don't love you because you do chores, or because of anything else you do or don't do. I love you because you're my son—and nothing will ever change that."

That is exactly what God is trying to tell us.

Many of us are like that little boy—knowing God loves us, but thinking it is for all the wrong reasons. Our security with God is tied to our performance. And so, as soon as our performance invariably slips, we feel like God is mad at us. And even when we are performing well, we are still insecure because we know that we cannot possibly keep it up for long. Even if we could work hard forever, there is this vague sense that we are being used by God as slaves, and we start to resent him and the work he has called us to do. But, like the child with his parent in the above story, we have had a significant misunderstanding. God does not love us for what we do; he loves us for who we are.

For he chose us in him before the creation of the world

> to be holy and blameless in his sight. In love he predestined us to be adopted as his sons through Jesus Christ, in accordance with his pleasure and will—to the praise of his glorious grace, which he has freely given us in the One he loves. (Ephesians 1:4–6)

That is why God created us—to be his dearly loved children.

I will never forget what it was like to be lost and confused many years ago in college. I desperately wanted to know who I was, why I was here, and what my life was really all about. These are the major questions that haunt everyone. Many books have been written and numerous hypotheses suggested, but God's word gives us the truth in just a few simple, yet profound, verses of scripture:

> "The God who made the world and everything in it is the Lord of heaven and earth and does not live in temples built by hands. And he is not served by human hands, as if he needed anything, because he himself gives all men life and breath and everything else. From one man he made every nation of men, that they should inhabit the whole earth; and he determined the times set for them and the exact places where they should live. *God did this so that men would seek him and perhaps reach out for him and find him*, though he is not far from each one of us. 'For in him we live and move and have our being.' As some of your own poets have said, *'We are his offspring.'*" (Acts 17:24–28, emphasis added)

Did you catch it? "God did this so that men would seek him and perhaps reach out for him and find him...we are his offspring" (vv27–28). That is the meaning of life. That is why we were created: to have a relationship with God.

God alone is infinitely and ultimately satisfying. His perfect character fits our complex needs for love, security and significance perfectly. A relationship with him is what will finally satisfy us fully and completely. Simply put, the purpose of our existence is to be with God.

Our Purpose and Our Mission

But what about the Great Commission in Matthew 28? Jesus told the apostles just before he ascended into heaven, "Therefore go and make disciples of all nations, baptizing them in the name of the Father and of the Son and of the Holy Spirit, and teaching them to obey everything I have commanded you. And surely I am with you always, to the very end of the age" (Matthew 28:19–20). This passage describes our mission. This is our task. But it is not our ultimate purpose.

The apostle Paul spoke of both his mission (or task) *and* his purpose in his farewell speech to the Ephesian elders. He makes a distinction between the two:

> And now, compelled by the Spirit, I am going to Jerusalem, not knowing what will happen to me there. I only know that in every city the Holy Spirit warns me that prison and hardships are facing me. However, I consider my life worth nothing to me, if only I may *finish the race and complete the task the Lord Jesus has given me—the task of testifying to the gospel of God's grace.* (Acts 20:22–24, emphasis added).

Finishing the race of faith and being rewarded by eternity with God is our ultimate purpose. Testifying to the gospel of God's grace is the task (or mission) that God has given us to complete while we are here on this earth. Both are important. But if we confuse one with the other, problems will ensue.

If we falsely assume that our purpose is to make disciples, then we will make "growth" lord instead of making Jesus Lord. We will serve and honor the god of numerical growth, looking to this false idol to bring us security, confidence and fulfillment. And when it does not, we will feel used, disillusioned and jaded. Eventually we will burn out because the false god of growth has no power to renew us, sustain us or strengthen us.

We will also make other false assumptions about Christianity that follow from this erroneous starting point, like measuring everything we do by its evangelistic purpose and effectiveness. This only adds to the vague sense that we are not really intrinsically valuable, but only insofar as we help the church to grow in numbers.

We were created in God's image and likeness (Genesis 1:27), and the precious blood of Christ was paid for our ransom (1 Peter 1:18–19). Make no mistake about it—we have intrinsic value to God! But the false god of numerical growth will chew us up and spit us out because it only values us for our effectiveness, leaving us feeling used, abused and discarded.

If on the other hand, we falsely assume that our mission or task is to piously be with God, then other problems develop. We can become so caught up in our own relationship with God that we cease to show his love to others. An extreme example of this is various ascetic movements which have led to such bizarre behavior as men and women taking vows of silence for years at a time as they cloister themselves away in monasteries, far from the needs of other people. But does this pass the "What would Jesus do?" test, or even the common sense test? If we are not careful, we can eventually rationalize away our responsibility to evangelize a lost world because we think we are accomplishing the more noble work of drawing nearer and nearer to God. But the Bible remains clear: "For anyone who does not love his brother, whom he has seen, cannot love God, whom he has not seen. And he has given us this command: Whoever loves God must also love his brother" (1 John 4:20–21). Therefore, we must not make it our mission to simply draw nearer and nearer to God without taking seriously his commands to love a lost and dying world.

So our purpose is to be with God, and our mission is to make disciples.[1] If we make that distinction clear in our lives, it will heal many of our past hurts and do much to ensure a healthy future.

Being with God in Heaven

One day, the faith shall be sight. At some point the God of our prayers will stand before us, plain as day. One day we will be with God as we are now with each other—in the same realm. It is this hope that keeps us going and this hope that Paul found so very encouraging: "And so we will be with the Lord forever. Therefore encourage each other with these words" (1 Thessalonians 4:17–18).

I can't wait to be with God in that way, can you? He is everything we have always dreamed of and more: our knight in shining armor, our perfect heavenly Father, and our dearest confidant and friend. Being with God will undoubtedly become the crescendo moment of history's symphony. Every instrument will be on key, every player on the same sheet of music, and every listener summarily transported by the heavenly artistry of it all. And the music will never stop, the dance will never end, the party will go on forever! We will enjoy unhindered relationships, unfettered freedom and joyous celebration. Excitement, adventure and fun beyond our wildest dreams; action, drama and mystery beyond our furthest imaginations. It will be better than living out your favorite movie fantasy by far, because it won't be a movie at all, but the real thing. Being with God in this way is the pinnacle of life that all true Christians look forward to with great anticipation. It is the grand purpose for which we were created.

The apostle Paul was shown a vision of paradise that was so exquisite, he was not even permitted to tell us what it was like; so alluring that it motivated him to stay faithful to the end (2 Corinthians 12:2–4). He even longed to die in order to taste heaven's delights earlier: "I desire to depart and be with Christ, which is better by far" (Philippians 1:23). But it was revealed to him that God wanted him to stay on earth a little longer for the joy and progress of the saints (Philippians 1:25). What did Paul see? Whatever it was, Paul longed for it with great anticipation, and so should we, since God specifically designed it to be the perfect fit for us. Every desire will be fully satisfied, every longing completely fulfilled, and every dream dramatically realized…forever! (Read more about the joy of heaven in chapter 10.)

Being with God on Earth

While this exciting fulfillment of our deepest desires will only be experienced in heaven, the Bible assures us that we are given a little foretaste of it here on earth, through his Spirit, which he has given us "as a deposit, guaranteeing what is to come" (2 Corinthians 1:21–22). Our marriages are far from perfect, but they are better than they were before we were Christians because of the Spirit's power at work in our lives. Our characters are far from perfect, but they are better than ever because of the Spirit's work in our lives.

The same should be true of our peace, happiness and fulfillment. This is a process, the ongoing work of the Holy Spirit in our lives: "And we, who with unveiled faces all reflect the Lord's glory, are being transformed into his likeness with ever-increasing glory, which comes from the Lord, who is the Spirit" (2 Corinthians 3:18).

And so the benefits of being with God have already begun for us here on earth:

> Though you have not seen him, you love him; and even though you do not see him now, you believe in him and are filled with an inexpressible and glorious joy, for you are receiving the goal of your faith, the salvation of your souls. (1 Peter 1:8–9)

The Plan from the Beginning

God has always wanted to simply be with us. His plan from the very beginning was to lovingly form out of the earth soul mates that he could breathe his Spirit into and enjoy sweet fellowship with forever. God put Adam and Eve into a garden paradise, replete with luscious fruit, a flowing river and precious stones of gold and onyx (Genesis 2:8–12). And in chapter 3 of Genesis we find God "walking in the garden in the cool of the day" (Genesis 3:8). It is not hard to imagine what it must have been like in those early days of the garden: Adam and Eve running around naked and carefree in paradise, frolicking with the friendly animals and running up to the Lord like little kids with their loving father as they strolled hand in hand through the fields together.

One of my favorite prayer-walk songs captures the spirit of this kind of fellowship with God that we all long for. Let the words call to you, as only longing words can do:

My God and I

My God and I go in the fields together.
We walk and talk as good friends should and do.
We clasp our hands; our voices ring with laughter.
My God and I walk through the meadow's hue.

He tells me of the years that went before me,
when heavenly plans were made for me to be.
When all was but a dream of dim conception,
to come to life, earth's verdant glory see.

My God and I will go for aye together.
We'll walk and talk as good friends should and do.
This earth will pass, and with it common trifles,
but God and I will go unendingly.

This earth will pass, and with it common trifles,
but God and I will go unendingly.[2]

Praise God, through Jesus Christ we can have this kind of walk with God today! I hope you are enjoying this kind of intimacy with God on a regular basis in your own life. If you are not, then know that God is waiting just outside the door of your heart, knocking and wanting to be invited in (Revelation 3:20). Don't wait any longer! Go pray to God and tell him you want to be heart-close again. He's just dying to be with you! (John 3:16).

God's Eternal Purpose

Unfortunately Adam and Eve's idyllic walk with God was abruptly aborted by the devastating intrusion of sin (Genesis 3:6). Adam and Eve disobeyed God by eating the one fruit they were forbidden to eat, and immediately their naïve nakedness turned to shameful nakedness, and the cycle of fear, shame and hiding was born.

But God promised that one day a descendant of Eve would come who would crush the head of the serpent that deceived them, even while his own heel would be struck—this was the first prophecy of the coming of Jesus Christ (Genesis 3:15, Hebrews 2:14).

Thus the course of human history becomes the dramatic backdrop for God's passionate story to unfold. God's people play the part of the wayward wife, torn between her love for God and her lust for the world (Hosea 1–14, Ezekiel 16). God himself plays the central character, the jilted lover who alternately expresses deep feelings of hurt, anger, love and forgiveness throughout the emotional roller coaster of their relationship. Satan is the cunning enemy who plots, schemes and plans to foil the lovers. Jesus is the hero, the fulfillment of prophecy who finally comes to destroy the devil's work and bridge the gap between God and man (1 John 3:8, Colossians 2:13–15). The Bible is one huge, beautiful love story.

The mission of the church is to make known this glorious story of God's eternal purpose. Read carefully as Paul puts our mission and our purpose into their proper perspective and right relationship in this short passage of Scripture that is just pregnant with insight:

> His intent was that now, through the church, the manifold wisdom of God should be made known to the rulers and authorities in the heavenly realms, according to his eternal purpose which he accomplished in Christ Jesus our Lord. In him and through faith in him we may

approach God with freedom and confidence. (Ephesians 3:10–12)

God has always intended for our purpose to drive our mission, not the other way around. A man without a purpose will never fulfill his mission. And a man without a mission does not understand his purpose. They are inextricably bound in God's eternal plan.

I Want to Be Like Jesus

Notice too the crucial role that Jesus Christ plays in our relationship with God the Father: "...according to his eternal purpose which he accomplished in Christ Jesus our Lord. In him and through faith in him we may approach God with freedom and confidence" (Ephesians 3:11–12). Jesus is "the way, the truth and the life" (John 14:6). He is the human bridge back to our divine father (1 Timothy 2:5–6). He is the sacred portal to the invisible realm of the spirit. He is the passageway to eternity. So, if we are to draw closer to God, it must be through faith in Jesus Christ.

The Bible directs us to focus on Jesus (Colossians 3:1–4). And as we focus on Jesus, we not only draw closer to God, but we also are slowly and miraculously transformed into his likeness with ever increasing glory, which comes from the Spirit working in our hearts (2 Corinthians 3:18). That too is the ultimate purpose of God for our lives: to be conformed to the likeness of God's son, Jesus Christ (Romans 8:28–29).

Thus, God's eternal plan and ultimate purpose for our lives is more fully explained as to be with God, through Jesus Christ, and become like him. These three elements of our ultimate purpose in life (to be with God, through Jesus Christ, and to be transformed into his likeness) are all interrelated. See how the following verse puts them together:

> But our citizenship is in heaven. And we eagerly await a Savior from there, the Lord Jesus Christ, who, by the

> power that enables him to bring everything under his
> control, will transform our lowly bodies so that they will
> be like his glorious body. (Philippians 3:20–21)

It makes sense. We are God's offspring (Acts 17:28); we are God's dearly loved children, whom he wants to grow up to be with him and like him (Ephesians 5:1–2). It is this hope that should motivate us to purify ourselves from sin on a daily basis:

> Dear friends, now we are children of God, and what we
> will be has not yet been made known. But we know that
> when he appears, we shall be like him, for we shall see
> him as he is. Everyone who has this hope in him purifies
> himself, just as he is pure. (1 John 3:2–3)

Thus, spiritual maturity is becoming more and more like Jesus. (Ephesians 4:13).

Most of us probably don't think enough about Jesus Christ throughout our day. Paul thought about him all the time. He said, "For me, to live is Christ, and to die is gain" (Philippians 1:21). In fact, Paul was so focused on Christ in his everyday life and speech that in his letter to the Philippian church, he mentions the words "Jesus," "Christ" or "Lord" seventy-five times in a hundred and four verses! Wow, that is a lot—Paul really had Jesus on his heart! He focused on Jesus in his everyday life. And he spoke about Jesus all the time, because out of the overflow of the heart, the mouth speaks (Luke 6:45).

The early church preached Jesus as their evangelistic message (Acts 2:22–36; 3:13–26; 4:8–12; 8:35; 10:34–43; 13:38–41; 17:1–3, 22–31; 22:6–21; 24:24; 26:9–23; 28:31). So must we. The early church held up Jesus in their discipling of one another (Colossians 1:28–29). So must we. The early church drew near to God through Jesus (Hebrews 4:14–16). So must we.

If we want to be with God, it is going to happen through Jesus Christ. Be eager to learn more about Jesus. Make him your hero. Make him your goal. And you will enjoy the close relationship with God that your soul longs for.

Hanging Out with God

Ever notice how you can just hang out with your best friend, and it doesn't matter what you are doing, as long as you are together? That is the kind of friendship God wants to have with us; where we can "be joyful always, pray continually and give thanks in all circumstances" (1 Thessalonians 5:16–18) just because we are together.

Paul said, "Rejoice in the Lord always. I will say it again: Rejoice!…The Lord is near" (Philippians 4:4–5). The basis of our rejoicing is that God is near! Living for our purpose is not just morally correct, it is emotionally fulfilling. How could we find a better friend than God himself? He is there for us through thick and thin. He is our faithful friend and companion along life's pilgrim journey. Read the words of another familiar devotional song that articulates these desires:

I Want Jesus to Walk with Me

I want Jesus to walk with me.
I want Jesus to walk with me.
All along life's pilgrim journey,
I want Jesus to walk with me.

In my trials, he'll walk with me.
In my sorrows, he'll walk with me.
All along life's pilgrim journey,
I want Jesus to walk with me.

Just as we want God to be with us, so God wants us to be with him. So, go ahead, have a cup of coffee with God. Listen to a song on the radio together. Invite him into your family time as you watch television together (you may find yourself turning away from more commercials and being a little more sensitive to your purity—amen!). Redefine your relationship with God from a half-hour prayer/Bible reading slot in the morning, to an awareness of his presence throughout the day that fills your life with awe and wonder!

Maybe it is time to reexamine the content of your prayer life. Do you like for people to be "all business" all the time? Of course not, and neither does God. So, why do we come to him with the same old prayer lists that bore him as much as they do us? Go for a run with God, watch a movie together, stroll through an art gallery if that is your cup of tea. Do something that is genuinely enjoyable to you, and it will be genuinely enjoyable to him.

David understood this, even though his wife did not:

> As the ark of the LORD was entering the City of David, Michal daughter of Saul watched from a window. And when she saw King David leaping and dancing before the LORD, she despised him in her heart. (2 Samuel 6:16)

David was leaping and dancing before God because…he felt like it! It wasn't a ritual, a tradition or a group exercise. It was just something fun to do with God. What do you feel like doing with God? Go do it, and watch your relationship with God come alive again!

Sometimes I like to go out and listen to a music CD with God. Other times I pray out loud as I am walking by my favorite lake. And still other times we just sit in silence together as I take in the beauty of his creation. Sometimes I pray through the outline of the Lord's prayer in Luke 11:2–4, or follow a simple outline of "praise and thanksgiving, confession and petition" in order to structure my thoughts. There is certainly nothing wrong with structure, but just remember that as the scaffolding is not the building, so the structure is not the prayer. Jesus said it was not the amount of words in your prayer that matter, but the amount of prayer in your words (Matthew 6:7).

I love to be with God. It is my favorite thing to do in life. It makes me happy just to think of him. He is everything to me;

everything I have always dreamed of. Isn't that the spirit of so many of the Psalms?

> Because your love is better than life,
>   my lips will glorify you....
> My soul will be satisfied as with the richest of foods.
> (Psalm 63:3,5a)

> Whom have I in heaven but you?
>   And earth has nothing I desire besides you....
> But as for me, it is good to be near God....
> (Psalm 73:25, 28a)

"But as for me, it is good to be near God...." I hope you feel that way too because that is the purpose for which you were created, the hope of heaven, and the joy of eternity—to be with God forever!

It's All About Love

God adores us, and he wants us to adore him. God enjoys spending time with us, and he wants us to enjoy spending time with him. God smiles when he thinks about us, and he wants us to smile when we think about him. Loving God and being loved by him is what life is all about:

> *And the prophets howl,*
> *   while the wise man cries:*
> *"It's all about love,*
> *   and the rest is all lies."*

A good friend of mine taught me a song many years ago that has become one of my favorites; it taps into our deepest desires to be with God:

Lonely Mountain

O Lord, I thought the day would never come
when I could lay my burdens down and walk with you.
But this morning as I greet the rising sun,
the fondest of my dreams have all come true.

O Lord, I need a mountain to climb on
Just a quiet place to go and know you're there.
O Lord, I need to spend some time with you.
Jesus spent the night with you in prayer.

The greatest friend you'll ever find
is on a lonely mountain.
The highest high you'll ever reach
is when you kneel to pray.
The brightest light you'll ever see
is when you close your eyes.
O Lord, you are my first love, at last I realize.

Somewhere in God's "art gallery" hangs this painting.

O Victory Sweet!

A dark night
on canvas, painted bright
with fireworks like
   Christmas lights
shooting, streaming
   everywhere—
like carousels
at every fair!

At center stands
a Knight of Light
with sword waved high
against the sky
as if to cry:
"O victory sweet!

"We vanquished he,
   who slain, now lies
beneath my feet!
   Prince of Darkness,
strong and sleek—
but tonight he lies
in crushed defeat!"

"Another day!"
Darkness shouts aloud.
But he can't be heard
   above the crowd
of singing saints
encircling he
who, washed, now stands
   both clean and free!

And to the chorus
   of the crowd
   the angels add
their voices loud:
"Another soul is won today!"

While on God's throne,
on the edge of his seat,
God reaches down,
   their hands to meet.
And, oh, the look
   in the Master's eyes
when we fight his fight
   and the saints baptize!

—Jeff Chacon

5

O VICTORY SWEET!

The Value of One Soul

Do you remember what it was like to be spiritually lost? Do you remember when life seemed like an unsolvable puzzle or maybe even a cruel joke? Do you remember waking up in the morning and dreading the day or going to bed at night and feeling that vague sense of emptiness because nothing ever seemed to satisfy as much as advertised?

I do. I remember feeling so lost and alone that it hurt. I remember tossing and turning in my bed with nightmares of losing control because I simply had nothing to hang on to. I remember coming home from the parties and feeling disappointed because yet another set of promises failed to materialize. As the Bob Seger song says, I was "young, restless and bored," and as the scripture says, I was "separate from Christ, excluded from citizenship in Israel and [foreigner] to the covenants of the promise, without hope and without God in the world" (Ephesians 2:12).

Do you remember? I hope so. I hope you never forget. The apostle Peter makes the argument that if a disciple is not growing spiritually it is because he is "nearsighted and blind, and has *forgotten* that he has been cleansed of his past sins" (2 Peter 1:9, emphasis added). We can never forget our past. We must always remember what it was like to be lost, so that we can praise God, thank him continually, and in response, have a heart that reaches to save one more.

God Is So Good!

Psalm 107 is one of those passages of scripture that I keep coming back to again and again in my Christian life; it reminds me what it was like to be lost and how thankful I am to be saved:

> Give thanks to the LORD, for he is good;
>> his love endures forever.
> Let the redeemed of the LORD say this—
>> those he redeemed from the hand of the foe,
> those he gathered from the lands,
>> from east and west, from north and south.
> (Psalm 107:1– 3)

God is so good! His love lasts forever! And who knows this better than the redeemed (or rescued) of the Lord—those God rescued from the hand of the foe and gathered from the lands? We have seen him at work in our own lives. We have witnessed his divine power as he stepped in at just the right time and hero-ically saved us from the jaws of death as they began to dig their pointed teeth into us. We narrowly escaped death, some of us physically or emotionally, and all of us spiritually. Praise God for his goodness and love.

The Psalm goes on to describe four different types of people who were in desperate straits, called out to God and were res-cued by him. See which of them you can identify with the most.

The Wanderer

> Some *wandered* in desert wastelands,
>> finding no way to a city where they could settle.
> They were hungry and thirsty,
>> and their lives ebbed away. (Psalm 107:4–5,
> emphasis added)

Can you relate to this passage? What was it like to wander from one relationship to the next, or from one job to the next, or from one obsession to the next, until you felt like you were in a desert wasteland that just went on forever and ever, with no settlement in sight? The Wanderer felt that gnawing hunger inside but did not know how to feed it; he felt that deep thirst in his soul, but did not know how to quench it. And so he just wandered from one disappointment to the next, and watched his life slowly slip away.

Remember when our lives were all about just going to work and collecting our pay, and going from thing to thing, day after day? They were pointless! Meaningless! I'm reminded of the book of Ecclesiastes where the writer expresses the frustration of a life apart from God when he says exasperatedly: "So I hated life, because the work that is done under the sun was grievous to me. All of it was meaningless, a chasing after the wind" (Ecclesiastes 2:17). Peter calls it "the empty way of life handed down to you from your forefathers" (1 Peter 1:18). Pointless! Meaningless! Empty! That is what it felt like for many of us who can relate to the Wanderer before we became Christians. We must never forget that feeling if we are to remain grateful to God in the long run.

The Psalm goes on to say,

> Then they cried out to the LORD in their trouble,
>   and he delivered them from their distress.
> He led them by a straight way
>   to a city where they could settle.
> Let them give thanks to the LORD for his unfailing love
>   and his wonderful deeds for men,
> for he satisfies the thirsty
>   and fills the hungry with good things.
> (Psalm107:6–9)

Give thanks to the Lord, for he is good.

The Rebel

> Some sat in darkness and the deepest gloom,
>   prisoners suffering in iron chains,
> for they had *rebelled* against the words of God
>   and despised the counsel of the Most High.
> So he subjected them to bitter labor;

> they stumbled and there was no one to help. (Psalm
> 107:10–12, emphasis added)

Maybe you can relate more to the Rebel than the Wanderer. Whereas the Wanderer roams aimlessly, the Rebel digs his heels in stubbornly. Whereas the Wanderer is lost in his search for fulfillment, the Rebel is imprisoned by his anger and resentment. The Rebel has a chip on his shoulder; he would rather fight than run, argue than settle, and brood than let go. He may appear fine on the outside, but inside he is sitting in darkness and the deepest gloom, a prisoner of his own bitterness, criticalness and hopelessness. The real problem is that he is fighting against God; happiness will never come because God does not give in to our pouting. God disciplines us in his love in order to break us of our rebellious pride and bring us to a point of surrender and spiritual desperation that brings us to turn humbly to him and his people for help.

> Then they cried out to the LORD in their trouble,
>   and he saved them from their distress.
> He brought them out of darkness and the deepest gloom
>   and broke away their chains.
> Let them give thanks to the LORD for his unfailing love
>   and his wonderful deeds for men,
> for he breaks down gates of bronze
>   and cuts through bars of iron. (Psalm 107:13–16)

Remember when you finally broke and gave in to God? The arm wrestling match was over; God won and you went home the winner. It felt so good to not be angry all the time inside anymore. The little irritations of life may still get to you once in a while, but you're basically at peace with the world—no longer the fighter, no longer the bad boy, and no longer the rebel. All that's left are the broken chains at your feet—a dramatic reminder of the power of God who "breaks down gates of bronze and cuts through bars of iron."

Let them give thanks to the Lord for his unfailing love and his wonderful deeds for men.

The Fool

> Some became *fools* through their rebellious ways
>   and suffered affliction because of their iniquities.
> They loathed all food
>   and drew near the gates of death. (Psalm
> 107:17–18, emphasis added)

The Fool was the life of the party for a while: happy-go-lucky and carefree, he seemed to have the world by the tail. But his fleeting happiness was based on a shallow and sinful lifestyle, a house of cards that was destined to crumble, because "God cannot be mocked. A man reaps what he sows. The one who sows to please his sinful nature, from that nature will reap destruction" (Galatians 6:7). Once the cards came crashing down, depression was soon to follow: "They loathed all food and drew near the gates of death" (v18). Eventually our sins have consequences: immorality leads to broken relationships and hurt feelings; impurity leads to dissatisfaction and emptiness; deceit gets exposed and destroys trust; and hedonism leads to self-loathing.

I know because this is my character: the Fool. I had to learn the hard way that cheap thrills are not cheap at all, but more costly than I could have ever imagined. I still regret the pain that I caused my disposable relationships, built on nothing more than mutual pleasure. My partying ways left me empty and dissatisfied, and soon the only thing I wanted in life was peace for my tortured and tormented soul:

> Then they cried to the LORD in their trouble,
>   and he saved them from their distress.
> He sent forth his word and healed them;
>   he rescued them from the grave. (Psalm 107:19–20)

I remember dropping to my knees every night before I went to bed for nine straight months my sophomore year of college and saying the same thing, "God, I don't know you, but I know you're there. Please, help me! Give me peace of mind!" Little did

I know that God had allowed me to hit rock bottom. I needed
to cry out to him in brokenness of heart and be spiritually prepared for one of his chosen servants to come and invite me to
church, where Jesus would save my soul and change my life forever:

> He sent forth his word and healed them;
>   he rescued them from the grave.
> Let them give thanks to the LORD for his unfailing love
>   and his wonderful deeds for men.
> Let them sacrifice thank offerings
>   and tell of his works with songs of joy. (Psalm
> 107:20–22)

God healed my soul and gave me the peace that I so desperately sought more than twenty years ago. He rescued me from
the grave, and I am forever indebted to him for it. I plan to
spend the rest of my days doing what he says to do in verse 22
above: "Let them sacrifice thank offerings and tell of his works
with songs of joy." How about you?

The Merchant

> Others went out on the sea in ships;
>   they were *merchants* on the mighty waters. (Psalm
> 107:23, emphasis added)

Perhaps you have viewed the first three types of people with
a slight disdain (though you would never admit it!). After all,
the Wanderer does not know what he wants; the Rebel is fool-
ishly destroying any chance he has for success, and the Fool is
frittering his life away on pleasure. The Merchant sees all of this
as weakness! He knows exactly what he wants in life, is hell-
bent on getting it, and sees other people as assets or liabilities
along the way. Ah, yes, the Merchant decided long ago what
would bring him happiness and fulfillment, and no one is going
to pull a fast one on him by preaching something about the love
of money being a root of all kinds of evil (1 Timothy 6:10). The
only people that say that, he reasons, are those that do not have

any. Can you relate to this one at all? If you are a saved Merchant, then you can also relate to the next verse:

> They saw the works of the LORD,
>   his wonderful deeds in the deep.
> For he spoke and stirred up a tempest
>   that lifted high the waves.
> They mounted up to the heavens and went down to the
>   depths;
>   in their peril their courage melted away.
> They reeled and staggered like drunken men;
>   they were at their wits' end. (Psalm 107:24–27)

God has designed life to be overwhelming, even for the Merchant, so that eventually he lies flat on his back looking up. God awaits his humble prayers. What was it that finally got to you, Merchant? Was it the stock market crashing? Or perhaps a neglected spouse or child who finally said, "Enough"? What got to your heart? What did God use to bring you to him? Do you remember? Does it still move your heart?

> Then they cried to the LORD in their trouble,
>   and he brought them out of their distress.
> He stilled the storm to a whisper;
>   the waves of the sea were hushed.
> They were glad when it grew calm,
>   and he guided them to their desired haven.
> Let them give thanks to the LORD for his unfailing love
>   and his wonderful deeds for men.
> Let them exalt him in the assembly of the people
>   and praise him in the council of the elders.
> (Psalm 107:28–32)

Whichever personality type you can relate to, God wants all of us to remember what it was like to be lost, what it took to be saved, and what we said we would always do as a result: praise and thank God the rest of our lives and never tire of telling others about him.

Are you still praising God for your salvation? Are you still telling others about him? I am determined to "let no debt remain outstanding, except the continuing debt to love one another" (Romans 13:8).

There are still a lot of lost people out there—Wanderers that are still wandering, Rebels that are still rebelling, Fools that are still philandering, and Merchants that are still worshiping money. And God cares for each one of them as much as he cares for each one of us.

Harassed and Helpless

> Jesus went through all the towns and villages, teaching in their synagogues, preaching the good news of the kingdom and healing every disease and sickness. When he saw the crowds, he had compassion on them, because they were *harassed and helpless*, like sheep without a shepherd. Then he said to his disciples, "The harvest is plentiful but the workers are few. Ask the Lord of the harvest, therefore, to send out workers into his harvest field." (Matthew 9:35–38, emphasis added)

How did Jesus view the crowds? Did he see them as a bother, an inconvenience or a burden? No, when Jesus looked out at the crowd of people around him, he thought about their lost condition spiritually and it moved him to compassion. He wasn't down on them or irritated by them because he saw them as victims of a world "under the control of the evil one" (1 John 5:19). He saw them as lost sheep, harassed and helpless, needing someone to show them the way home.

I remember when I saw the crowds that way too. I often could not walk past strangers without asking myself if they knew God or not. Every stadium filled with people was a vision of how the church would someday look when thousands were true disciples of Jesus. And every daily interaction was a new opportunity to share my faith with someone that the Lord had obviously directed my way.

But to keep that heart of love and hope for the world around me has proven to be a more difficult task then I ever imagined.

It seems that when I was young in the Lord, evangelism was new and exciting—a fresh idea that I enjoyed carrying out with zeal and enthusiasm. I enjoyed the real life drama and adventure of sharing the gospel with someone that I was sure God had prepared to hear it. I especially loved (and still do love) the thrill of seeing the lights come on for the very first time in someone's thinking about Jesus dying on the cross for their sins personally. I loved seeing them grasp how much they are loved by God and how desperately God wants them to repent of their sins and find the life that he has wanted to give them from the beginning of time. And then to watch them be immersed in water for the forgiveness of their sins and to receive the Holy Spirit and a place among the redeemed (Acts 2:38–41). That is exciting stuff to be a part of! And that stuff still thrills my soul today.

But I have found that our enemy is more formidable than I ever imagined. His constant attacks on us "soldiers of light" have left all of us bleeding, many of us maimed, and still others destroyed completely. To be sure, in any war there are casualties, but who of us thought we would be one of them? The war to free men's souls from "the power of Satan to God" (Acts 26:18) has left many of us freedom fighters worn and weary. We are desperate for encouragement, needing faith, hope and love to replenish our souls.

Paul urges us, "Let us not become weary in doing good, for at the proper time we will reap a harvest if we do not give up" (Galatians 6:9).

The writer of Hebrews similarly encourages us with these words:

> Remember those earlier days after you had received the light, when you stood your ground in a great contest in the face of suffering. Sometimes you were publicly exposed to insult and persecution; at other times you stood side by side with those who were so treated. You sympathized with those in prison and joyfully accepted the confiscation of your property, because you knew that

you yourselves had better and lasting possessions.

So do not throw away your confidence; it will be richly rewarded. You need to persevere so that when you have done the will of God, you will receive what he has promised. For in just a very little while,

> "He who is coming will come and will not delay.
>> But my righteous one will live by faith.
> And if he shrinks back,
>> I will not be pleased with him."

But we are not of those who shrink back and are destroyed, but of those who believe and are saved. (Hebrews 10:32–39)

There are so many scriptures that are written to strengthen the weary warrior and encourage us to take heart and keep fighting the good fight of faith (1 Timothy 6:12–16). In fact Romans 15:4–5 says that is one of the main purposes of the Scriptures themselves:

> For everything that was written in the past was written to teach us, so that through *endurance and the encouragement* of the Scriptures we might have hope.
>
> May the God who gives *endurance and encouragement* give you a spirit of unity among yourselves as you follow Christ Jesus. (emphasis added)

The Scriptures are so encouraging! And God is revealed here as one who gives endurance and encouragement through them. We've simply got to spend more time pouring the encouragement of the Scriptures into our hearts and into each other's hearts!

Watch how vital the Scriptures are to us according to the psalmist's meditation about the word of God in Psalm 119:

> My soul is weary with sorrow;
>> strengthen me according to your word. (v28)

> My comfort in my suffering is this:
>> Your promise preserves my life. (v50)

> If your law had not been my delight,

I would have perished in my affliction.
I will never forget your precepts,
for by them you have preserved my life. (vv92–93)

The unfolding of your words gives light;
it gives understanding to the simple. (v130)

Seven times a day I praise you
for your laws.
Great peace have they who love your law,
and nothing can make them stumble. (vv164–165)

The Scriptures are fuel for our engines, oil for our lamps and food for our souls. We are to feed on them as Jesus did in order to have the spiritual strength to fight off Satan's attacks and stay faithful to God in the long run (Matthew 4:1–4).

Dreaming for the Lost

When Jesus entered Jericho, he saw a most unusual sight: a well-dressed man who had climbed a sycamore-fig tree in order to get a better view of his entrance. Jesus must have been impressed and probably amused: "When Jesus reached the spot, he looked up and said to him, 'Zacchaeus, come down immediately, I must stay at your house today.' So he came down at once and welcomed him gladly" (Luke 19:5–6).

Zacchaeus, the wealthy chief tax collector, said to Jesus, "Look Lord! Here and now I give half of my possessions to the poor, and if I have cheated anybody out of anything, I will pay back four times the amount" (Luke 19:8). Well, you can imagine that people were almost falling over each other to form a line in front of the man who had surely cheated many in their town and was now promising to pay back four times the amount he had stolen from them! This was the best news the townspeople had heard in years!

Jesus himself was impressed with Zacchaeus. I imagine Jesus looking across the room at Zacchaeus and making eye contact with him amidst the stirring of people around them as he proclaimed with admiration in his voice: "Today salvation has come to this house, because this man, too, is a son of Abraham" (Luke 19:9).

Zacchaeus could have died and gone to heaven right then and there. The man he had admired enough to climb a tree to see was now telling him in front of everyone that he had a noble heart, and that he would be saved because he had the faith that was seen in his father Abraham.

But the happiest man in Jericho that day was not Zacchaeus or any of those who were lining up to collect their four times amount of money that had been stolen from them. It was the man whose gaze had not yet disengaged from the repentant tax collector as he marveled aloud, half to Zacchaeus and half to himself: "For the Son of Man came to seek and to save what was lost" (Luke 19:10).

I am sure there were a lot of reasons Jesus did what he did. But I just have to wonder if this wasn't the biggest one: seeing the miracle of a changed heart, as one who was lost and going to hell was now saved and going to heaven forever. It must have thrilled his heart to see one more soul saved from the penalty and power of sin. It must have made all the hassles with the Pharisees and all the misunderstandings of the crowd worth it— to see a man, made in the image of his heavenly Father, reconciled to God again (2 Corinthians 5:18–20). It was this joy that motivated our Lord to go all the way to the cross for us:

> Let us fix our eyes on Jesus, the author and perfecter of our faith, who for the joy set before him endured the cross, scorning its shame, and sat down at the right hand of the throne of God. Consider him who endured such opposition from sinful men, so that you will not grow weary and lose heart. (Hebrews 12:2–3)

The very heart of the Gospel message itself is that Jesus loved us so much that he was willing to lay down his life for us so that we could be reconciled to God:

> Once you were alienated from God and were enemies in

> your minds because of your evil behavior. But now he has
> *reconciled you by Christ's physical body through death*
> *to present you holy in his sight, without blemish and free*
> *from accusation.* (Colossians 1:21–22, emphasis added)

What fired Jesus up was his passion to save lost souls. Picture Jesus looking straight into your eyes as he says to you: "For the Son of Man came to seek and to save what was lost" (Luke 19:10). Aren't you glad Jesus saved your soul? Once again, don't you want to decide to be like him? "Come follow me," Jesus continues, "and I will make you fishers of men" (Mark 1:17). That is the dream that first ignited my soul. And that is the dream that still fires me up today.

One at a Time

The story is told of an old man who was watching a young boy on a beach picking up starfish, one at a time, and throwing them back into the sea. An unusually high tide had washed several thousand of them up onto the shore that morning, and now they were stranded on the beach, doomed to die under the dry heat of a midday sun. So the boy, taking pity on the starfish, was carefully picking them up, one by one, and tossing them back into the ocean so they could live.

The old man shook his head and scoffed in contempt at the boy's futile efforts to change an obviously hopeless situation. Finally, he walked over to the boy and knowingly posed his loaded question, "Son, do you really think you can make a difference by yourself out here with more starfish than you could possibly save in a year's time on this beach?"

The boy looked at the old man with a wisdom that comes not from age but from innocence, as he bent down and took hold of another starfish, wound up like a baseball pitcher and threw it as far as he could in the direction of the ocean. It landed with a slight splash and quickly sank to the bottom of the sea, disappearing from their sight. Then the boy turned to the old man and simply said: "I made a difference to that one."

I am glad a single professional man, who had become a Christian himself only six months earlier, decided to take an evening class at the University of San Diego in the spring of 1981. He made this decision for the express purpose of finding someone in that class who wanted to study the Bible and find God's will for his or her life. I found out later that he had invited every single one of my classmates before he finally invited me to his Thursday night Bible Study. All of them had politely turned him down; I said, "Yes," little knowing that this was the long-awaited answer to nine months of desperate prayer in the secrecy of my dorm room. Three months later I was baptized into Christ and my soul was saved, changing the course and destiny of my life forever.

I've often wondered in the years since then: "Did John have a great time with God the morning of the day that he shared his faith with me, or was he hurried and rushed that morning? Was John responding to a lesson on evangelism that he had heard at church that weekend, or was he involved in a special evangelistic campaign with his Bible Study group? Was he sharing his faith with me legalistically or from his heart? Did he have faith that I would come, or did he doubt in his heart my willingness? I mean, what motivated John to share with me that particular night when only God knew that I had been spiritually prepared to respond positively to an invitation to study the Bible at that particular time in my life?

The answer is...it doesn't really matter! John Godwin and I have been best friends for the last twenty-three years, ever since our first encounter after class that night on campus; and in all that time, I have never asked him what his motivation was for sharing his faith with me that monumental night in my life, because I don't care. The only thing I care about is that God used somebody willing to open his mouth to invite me to come and hear the gospel of the ages with the power to save my soul. That is all that matters to me!

You know what…even on a bad day, we can still share our faith with somebody who desperately needs a relationship with God. It is not about us. It is about them. We do not evangelize to accumulate brownie points in heaven. We evangelize because there are still billions of people out there who are lost and dying, just like we were—Wanderers still wandering; Rebels still rebelling; Fools still philandering, and Merchants still buying and selling. And like that young boy at the beach rescuing starfish from the scorching sun, we have the opportunity to rescue lost souls from hell, to make a difference in people's lives—one at a time.

Let's go save one more.

God's Search

I'm searching for a man
who is willing to believe
that greatness is given
to those who receive.

He must believe once again
that he can run with the horses
and call on God's power
to summon his forces.

I want a man
with a gleam in his eye—
with his feet on the ground
and his head in the sky.

Where is the man
who will forsake all others
for the love of his God
and the sake of his brothers?

Find me the man
who counts everything a loss—
save the message of Jesus
and his death on the cross!

I'm searching for a man
who knows who he is—
who will drive out demons
because the power is his.

Now I've caught your eye—
Are you the one?
Tell me you're willing
to follow my Son.

Are you the man
who is willing to be great—
who will overcome fear
for destiny's sake?

Remember who you are;
remember where you're from—
you're a man of God…
you are God's son!

—Jeff Chacon

6

GOD'S WARRIORS

We Were Destined to Dare Greatly

There is something deep inside of all of us that longs to do something great with our lives. We know that we are flawed; we know that we are weak, and we know that we have made more mistakes then we would ever like to admit. But still, we also know that something great resides in our hearts, just waiting for the right moment to burst onto the stage of life and make a real difference in this world.

William Wallace was a man of destiny. Born in 1272, the second of three sons to an obscure Scottish knight named Sir Malcolm Wallace, this courageous revolutionary leader, without the support of a single noble, rallied the Scottish peasants to gain their freedom from the cruel and ruthless rule of England under Edward the Longshanks. No one who has seen the movie *Braveheart* will ever forget the scene in which Wallace courageously goes to his death claiming freedom for his people. This story of bravery and commitment touches those sacred places in all of us and makes us yearn to do something great with our lives as well!

The fact is that we truly can be heroes and heroines on the stage of life since God designed it to be lived amidst the backdrop of a great battle. In fact, that is our destiny—to fight and win that battle!

Destiny

Remember the classic scene in the *Star Wars* movie when the evil Darth Vader is trying to lure the good Luke Skywalker over to "the dark side"? He says in the climactic scene of the movie in his trademark deep, raspy voice: "It is your destiny." Of course, Luke chooses against his evil father's persuasion and fights for the freedom fighters and the Federation on the side of light.

But the line remains a classic: "It is your destiny."

Have you ever wondered what your destiny is? Have you ever dreamed about it? As children, most of us wanted to be "one of the good guys": maybe a policeman, a fireman, a doctor or a nurse. I wanted to be like Captain Kirk on the Starship Enterprise, of the old *Star Trek* television series, or James West of the equally exciting television show *The Wild, Wild West*. When I read books, I was drawn to the noble chivalry of the Knights of the Round Table. When I started getting more into sports, I wanted to be like my childhood football hero, Lance Alworth, the acrobatic San Diego Charger wide receiver who could turn the course of a game with a single magnificent catch.

Who were your childhood heroes? Who did you want to be like? Chances are they were great in one way or another—larger than life characters who made a difference somehow in life.

As we got older, our heroes changed with us. Soon the definition of success evolved in our minds to something else, and we found ourselves admiring new heroes. Perhaps financial success captured our fancy, or professional success of one kind or another. Maybe a social or political leader stirred something inside of us. I remember having the good fortune of seeing the great Latino social and political leader, Cesar Chavez, speak at one of my father's political functions. As he stepped up to the podium to speak, it seemed to me that he had the spiritual power and presence of Mahatma Gandhi or Martin Luther King. I don't remember a word of what he said, but I remember his presence and thinking to myself: I want to be like that some day.

Many times in our adult years our dreams begin to fade as the cruel realities of life rob us of our hope. Soon our dreams turn to nightmares, and we begin to think in terms of what we hope our destiny is not! One woman's greatest fear is that she would not make it financially and become in her words, "a bag lady" who lived on the streets. As disciples, we can wonder if we are destined for moral failure. Will I end up being a Judas and betraying Jesus? Or perhaps like King Saul who started strong and then had the kingdom taken from him because of his disobedience to God? Maybe I will end up being a legalistic Pharisee who loses touch with the heart of God. Or even like the rich young ruler who walked away from Jesus when it counted the most.

Fortunately the Bible says that God has a great destiny and plan in store for each and every one of us: "'For I know the plans I have for you,' declares the LORD, 'plans to prosper you and not to harm you, plans to give you hope and a future'" (Jeremiah 29:11).

But it is up to us to fulfill that destiny, since God allows everyone the choice of fulfilling or rejecting his purpose for us: "But the Pharisees and experts in the law rejected God's purpose for themselves" (Luke 7:30).

Remember Who You Are

One of the reasons Disney's blockbuster movie *The Lion King* was such a smashing success with audiences of all ages is that it touched on spiritual themes that affect us deeply. Simba is the young lion cub whose destiny it is to be king some day. But he must learn to overcome the deceitful schemes of his evil uncle, Scar, and confront his own fears, doubts and failures in order to become the heir to the throne and fulfill his destiny. The pivotal scene in this movie is when the Zen-like baboon, Rafiki, leads the now grown Simba to a stream and has him peer into it and find the reflection of his deceased father, Mufasa. When all the disappointed young lion sees is his own reflection, the wise Rafiki urges him to "look harder," at which point Simba sees the similarities between himself and his father, and realizes that the heart of his father resides within him. Then Simba hears the voice of his father in a mystical interchange that reveals the secret to Simba fulfilling his destiny as the new lion king. His father tells him that he has forgotten who he is, and so he has forgotten who his father is. Then he says, "Remember who you are. You are my son, the one true king."

Like Simba, we are heirs to the throne as children of God, the King of the universe (Romans 8:17). But we have forgotten who we are and where we came from. We too must look inside ourselves to see the image of God in which we were created. We are more than what we have become. We too must take our rightful place in the circle of life and for all eternity. But our past failures haunt us; we, like Simba, are afraid that we are not who we used to be when we were young and idealistic. But God, speaking to us in much the same way that Mufasa spoke to Simba, reminds us in the crucial scene of our own stories: "Remember who you are. You are my son."

What's in a Name?

> Abram fell facedown, and God said to him, "As for me, this is my covenant with you: You will be the father of many nations. *No longer will you be called Abram; your name will be Abraham, for I have made you a father of many nations.* I will make you very fruitful; I will make nations of you, and kings will come from you." (Genesis 17:3–6, emphasis added)

When God renames someone, it changes his or her destiny forever. In the above verse, God in effects says,

1. Here is who you will be some day ("father of many nations").
2. So, I am going to call you that from now on (the name "Abraham" means "father of many nations").

3. And I promise you that it will occur just as I said it would. In, fact, in my mind, it has already occurred ("for I have made you a father of many nations").

The God who "gives life to the dead and calls things that are not as though they were" (Romans 4:17) has just created a new reality for Abraham. For his part, all Abraham has to do is believe what God has said about him—and his name has been changed to remind him.

And that is exactly what God has done with us!

Just as Abram's name was changed to Abraham before he even had a single son, and Simon's name was changed to Peter before he became a rock in the faith, and Gideon was proclaimed a "Mighty Warrior" before he ever led the Israelites into battle—so we are given several names in the Bible by God before we ever do anything great in order to inspire us to become all that God envisions us to be. We just need to believe it.

Who We Are in Christ

It is so exciting to go through your Bible and highlight scriptures that reveal all the names you can find that God has given us in Christ. Just let the Holy Spirit encourage your soul as you read this partial list of the names that God has given to us as Christians:

Ambassadors of Christ (2 Corinthians 5:20)
Anointed of God (2 Corinthians 1:21)
Appointed for eternal life (Acts 13:48)
Aroma of Christ (2 Corinthians 2:15)
Believers (Acts 2:44)
Body of Christ (1 Corinthians 12:27)
Branches (John 15:5)
Bride of Christ (2 Corinthians 11:2, Revelation 19:7)
Brothers of Jesus (Hebrews 2:11)
(The) Called (Jude 1, Revelation 17:14)
Children of God (1 John 3:1)

Children of Light (Ephesians 5:8)
Christians (Acts 11:26; 1 Peter 4:16)
(The) Chosen (Revelation 17:14)
(A) Chosen people (1 Peter 2:9)
Church of Christ (Romans 16:16)
Church of God (1 Corinthians 1:2; 2 Corinthians 1:1)
Church of the firstborn (Hebrews 12:23)
City of the living God (Hebrews 12:22)
Disciples (Acts 11:26)
Faithful followers (Revelation 17:14)
(The) Faithful in Christ Jesus (Ephesians 1:1)
Family of God (1 Peter 4:17)
Friends (3 John 14)
Friends of Jesus (John 15:15)
God's fellow workers (1 Corinthians 3:9)
God's field (1 Corinthians 3:9)
God's building (1 Corinthians 3:9)
God's elect (Titus 1:1; 1 Peter 1:1)
Heirs of God (Romans 8:17)
Holy and faithful brothers in Christ (Colossians 1:2)
Holy nation (1 Peter 2:9)
Holy priesthood (1 Peter 2:5)
Light of the world (Matthew 5:14)
Men sent from God (2 Corinthians 2:17)
People belonging to God (1 Peter 2:9)
People of God (1 Peter 2:10)
Royal priesthood (1 Peter 2:9)
Salt of the earth (Matthew 5:13)
Saints in Christ Jesus (Philippians 1:1)
Servants of Christ (1 Corinthians 4:1, Philippians 1:1)
Slaves of Christ (Ephesians 6:6)
Soldiers of Christ Jesus (2 Timothy 2:3)
Sons of the day (1 Thessalonians 5:5)
Sons of the light (1 Thessalonians 5:5)
Sons of the living God (Romans 9:26)

Which name do you like best on this list? Is there one that really fires you up? Go ahead; try it on for size. Call yourself that name and let it sink in. That is who you really are in the eyes of God! That is the plan of God and the destiny God has for your life.

The Power of a Name

We must shed the past labels that have shackled us for years: "Failure," "Loser," "Choker," etc. These are the names that Satan wants to continually beat us down with, but God has already proclaimed us to be winners in Christ, and it is up to us to believe it. Watch how calling ourselves one of the names that God has given to us (in the following example, "servants"), actually affects our view of ourselves and how others view us:

> So then, men ought to regard us as servants of Christ and as those entrusted with the secret things of God. (1 Corinthians 4:1)

> For we do not preach ourselves, but Jesus Christ as Lord, and ourselves as your servants for Jesus' sake. (2 Corinthians 4:5)

> Paul and Timothy, servants of Christ Jesus... (Philippians 1:1)

> Live as free men, but do not use your freedom as a cover-up for evil; live as servants of God. (1 Peter 2:16)

Notice that the new name, "servant" in this case, communicates volumes to us about who Paul and Timothy are, how they view themselves, and how the Christians they were writing to viewed and received them as well. The simple use of a name communicates something very important about their identity in Christ.

A few years ago, a good friend of mine was struggling with his identity and role in the church. He had been promised a leadership role that never materialized, and it left him feeling disappointed and a little confused about God's plan for his life. He knew that he was saved and loved by God, but he didn't know where he fit into the Lord's church—what was his role, what was his calling, and what was his destiny? In an effort to encourage him I wrote the following poem. I offer it here as an encouragement to others who may be able to relate to this same struggle, and also as another example of the power in a name.

The Question

*Who knows, who cares, who wonders who they'll be
when life is a lark and all is carefree?*

*But something changes deep inside
when the Great One calls and there's nowhere to hide.*

*First fear, then resistance, then soon we give in.
And the question is born: "Where do I fit in?"*

*I asked for a sword, and was given a towel.
I asked to lead and was told to follow.*

*So I followed closely and gave my heart.
I washed feet that were dirty and did my part.*

*And there were times of blessing that could not be denied,
and times of testing that I cried and cried.*

*Then one day it was over in the twinkling of an eye,
and all that were dead were again alive.*

*And the Great One came to the back of the line
and said, "You come first. You there, you're mine."*

*Then the towel in my hand became a great sword
with the words in blood: "Jesus is Lord!"*

*And the question was answered: "Where do I fit in?"
"I'm a humble servant, a servant of him."*

—Jeff Chacon

Born to Be like Jesus

If hearing the Lord call your name and remembering who you are in Christ is exciting, then how about envisioning who you will become some day? Not only does God's word give us an exciting view of our present, but it also gives us an absolutely thrilling picture of our future! See what the Holy Spirit tells us about our future glory through the letter of Paul to the Corinthians:

> So will it be with the resurrection of the dead. The body that is sown is perishable, it is raised imperishable; it is sown in dishonor, it is raised in glory; it is sown in weakness, it is raised in power; it is sown a natural body, it is raised a spiritual body. (1 Corinthians 15:42–44)

The Bible teaches that our physical bodies are merely the seeds of something far greater and more magnificent than any body we could possibly imagine. As an orange seed to an orange, or a human embryo to a human being, so our current physical bodies pale in comparison with the eternal bodies God has planned for us. The verse above says that our physical bodies are perishable, but our eternal bodies will be imperishable; our physical bodies are dishonored, but our eternal bodies will be glorious; our physical bodies are weak, but our eternal bodies will be powerful; our physical bodies are made of dust, but our eternal bodies will be made of spirit!

Will we fly among the stars and the planets as we sail the celestial winds of time with reckless abandon? Will we climb the heights of the highest mountains and swim to the depths of the deepest seas? Will we float on the notes of the most beautiful music and dance to the rhythms of the most exotic sounds? Who knows?! As the Bible says, "No eye has seen, no ear has heard, no mind has conceived what God has prepared for those who love him" (1 Corinthians 2:9). We just know that it will be everything we ever dreamed of and more. God definitely wants us to get excited about who he has predestined us to become one day! "And just as we have borne the likeness of the earthly man, so shall we bear the likeness of the man from heaven" (1 Corinthians 15:49).

The really exciting thing about all this is that one day we will reach our goal of Christ-likeness "in a flash, in the twinkling of an eye, at the last trumpet. For the trumpet will sound, the dead will be raised imperishable, and we will be changed" (1 Corinthians 15:52). Jesus is God in the flesh, and the Bible teaches us that some day we will finally become like him. What does that mean? It means that you and I were created for greater glory than we ever imagined. It means that we have been aiming too low; God has plans not just to adopt us as his spiritual children, but to make us heirs of all that he has:

> Because you are sons, God sent the Spirit of his Son into our hearts, the Spirit who calls out, "Abba, Father." So you are no longer a slave, but a son; and since you are a son, God has made you also an heir. (Galatians 4:6–7)

> Now if we are children, then we are heirs—heirs of God and co-heirs with Christ, if indeed we share in his sufferings in order that we may also share in his glory. (Romans 8:17)

We will some day share in the glory of Jesus Christ himself! Let us expand our minds a little bit and allow ourselves to dream about what that will be like. Let us think through who Jesus Christ really is and what names the Bible gives to him.

Who Is Jesus?

Here is a partial list of the names of Jesus Christ in the Bible:

Almighty (Revelation 1:8)
Alpha and the Omega (Revelation 1:8)
Author and perfecter of our faith (Hebrews 12:2)
Author of life (Acts 3:15)
Deliverer (Romans 11:26)
Faithful and True (Revelation 19:11)
Faithful witness (Revelation 1:5)
Firstborn from among the dead (Revelation 1:5)
God over all (Romans 9:5)
Heir of all things (Hebrews 1:2)
Holy and Righteous One (Acts 3:14)

I Am (John 8:58)
King of kings and Lord of lords (Revelation 19:16)
Light of the world (John 8:12)
Lion of Judah (Revelation 5:5)
Lord of all (Romans 10:12)
(The) Morning Star (Revelation 22:16; 2 Peter 1:19)
(The) One God loves (Ephesians 1:6)
Our hope (1 Timothy 1:1)
Prince and Savior (Acts 5:31)
Radiance of God's glory (Hebrews 1:3)
Resurrection and the life (John 11:25)
Ruler of the kings of the earth (Revelation 1:5)
Savior (2 Timothy 1:10, Titus 2:13)
Savior of the world (1 John 4:14)
Son God loves (Colossians 1:13)
Son of God (John 1:34, John 1:49)
(The) Way, the truth, and the life (John 14:6)
Word of God (John 1:1, 14; Revelation 19:13)

Jesus is everything we have always wanted to become. He is our hero, our goal and our destiny. When God created man in his own image and likeness (Genesis 1:26), he had more in mind than just giving us free will; he wants us to "participate in the divine nature" (2 Peter 1:4). All our desires for greatness have not been prideful after all; God himself has placed them there.

Overcoming Fear

All of this can be quite overwhelming to us flawed and failing human beings. We would like to believe in the identity and destiny that God has for us, but we wonder deep down if we have what it takes to become all of that.

Therefore it is important that when we are afraid, we remember a couple of essential Biblical truths that will drive away our fears. The first is that God is the one who will bring all of this to pass, not us. Consider the following passages that point to God's initiative and power in the process of perfecting us:

> He will keep you strong to the end, so that you will be blameless on the day of our Lord Jesus Christ. God, who has called you into fellowship with his Son Jesus Christ our Lord, is faithful. (1 Corinthians 1:8–9)

> May God himself, the God of peace, sanctify you through and through. May your whole spirit, soul and body be kept blameless at the coming of our Lord Jesus Christ. The one who calls you is faithful and he will do it. (1 Thessalonians 5:23–24)

> Being confident of this, that he who began a good work in you will carry it on to completion until the day of Christ Jesus. (Philippians 1:6)

Notice that it is not our power that will accomplish our salvation and transformation, but God's power.

A second important Biblical truth to remember is that we are not alone in this process; God has promised to accompany us on our journey. I recently did a study on "fear" in the Bible and noticed that the single greatest reassurance that God gives us in his word to help us overcome our fears is that he himself will be with us all along the way. Consider the following tender reassurances from the book of Isaiah designed to comfort and strengthen us when we're afraid:

> Strengthen the feeble hands,
>> steady the knees that give way;
> *say to those with fearful hearts,*
>> *"Be strong, do not fear;*
> *your God will come,*
>> he will come with vengeance;
> with divine retribution
>> he will come to save you." (Isaiah 35:3–4,
> emphasis added)

> *"So do not fear, for I am with you;*
>> do not be dismayed, for I am your God.
> I will strengthen you and help you;
>> *I will uphold you with my righteous right hand."*
> (Isaiah 41:10, emphasis added)

"For I am the LORD, your God,
    who takes hold of your right hand
and says to you, 'Do not fear';
    I will help you." (Isaiah 41:13, emphasis added)

But now, this is what the LORD says—
    he who created you, O Jacob,
    he who formed you, O Israel:
"Fear not, for I have redeemed you;
    I have summoned you by name; you are mine.
When you pass through the waters,
    I will be with you;
and when you pass through the rivers,
    they will not sweep over you.
When you walk through the fire,
    you will not be burned;
    the flames will not set you ablaze...
Do not be afraid, for I am with you." (Isaiah 43:1–2, 5,
emphasis added)

There is nothing to fear. God will keep us strong to the end, and he will be right there beside us the whole way.

So, in the words of William Shakespeare: "Be not afraid of greatness." It is your destiny.

God's Search

Do you remember who you are now? Have the Scriptures convinced you of your true identity and destiny yet? Will you overcome your fears in order to grab hold of the life that God is offering you? I hope so. You will be so much happier. You can do it. God is desperately searching the entire earth right now, looking for someone to strengthen who is willing to get up and try again: "For the eyes of the LORD range throughout the earth to strengthen those whose hearts are fully committed to him" (2 Chronicles 16:9). Are you willing to get up and try again? It is not too late. Dare to dream again about what God can do in your life!

Faith at the Door

Fear knocked at the door,
* and Faith answered it.*
*   But Faith found no one there—*
*   because Faith drives out Fear!*

Doubt and Insecurity knocked at the door,
* and Faith answered it.*
*   But Faith found no one there—*
*   because Faith drives out Doubt and Insecurity!*

Anxiety and Stress knocked at the door,
* and Faith answered it.*
*   But Faith found no one there—*
*   because Faith drives out Anxiety and Stress!*

Discouragement and Depression knocked at the door,
* and Faith answered it.*
*   But Faith found no one there—*
*   because Faith drives out Discouragement and*
*   Depression.*

Trial and Challenge knocked at the door,
* and Faith answered it…and let them in.*
*   They fellowshiped till the wee hours of the morning,*
*   until finally, Trial and Challenge left,*
*   and only Faith remained—*
*   stronger than ever before!*

—Jeff Chacon

7

FAITH AT THE DOOR

The Real Work of God Is to Believe

Jesus had just taken five small loaves of bread and two small fish and miraculously fed about 5,000 people (John 6:1–14). As a result, the crowd wanted to come and make him their king by force (v15), so Jesus slipped away from them to the other side of the lake. They hurriedly got into some boats and tried to find him, searching for the one who had given them what they wanted: food for their stomachs. But Jesus wanted to feed their souls. So, this encounter ensues:

> When they found him on the other side of the lake, they asked him, "Rabbi, when did you get here?"
>
> Jesus answered, "I tell you the truth, you are looking for me, not because you saw miraculous signs but because you ate the loaves and had your fill. Do not work for food that spoils, but for food that endures to eternal life, which the Son of Man will give you. On him God the Father has placed his seal of approval."
>
> Then they asked him, "What must we do to do the works God requires?"
>
> Jesus answered, "The work of God is this: to believe in the one he has sent." (John 6:25–29)

There are at least two lessons that Jesus is teaching. The first lesson is readily apparent: "Do not work for food that spoils, but for food that endures to eternal life" (v27). Jesus is urging them to listen to the hunger pangs of their souls and not try to satisfy that hunger with the bread of earth, but with the bread of heaven—Jesus Christ.

The second lesson may not be so obvious, but it is equally important: "Then they asked him, 'What must we do to do the works God requires?' Jesus answered, 'The work of God is this: to believe in the one he has sent'" (vv28–29).

For the people of his day, this may have been more difficult than for us 2,000 years later. They knew him not as the one they grew up worshiping and praying through, but rather as one of their neighbors who lived down the street: "At this the Jews began to grumble about him because he said, 'I am the bread that came down from heaven.' They said, 'Is this not Jesus, the son of Joseph, whose father and mother we know? How can he now say, "I came down from heaven?"'" (John 6:41–42). It must have been very difficult for them to swallow the idea that they must "feed on" this man who seemed to be just another human being like themselves.

But upon further reflection, it becomes clear that to believe in Jesus is much harder than we think, even for us today.

What Do You Believe?

Do you believe that without Jesus Christ, you have no life in you? (John 6:53). Do you believe that life apart from him is really no life at all? Do you believe that you need to feed on that life every day, just as you feed on physical food, in order to live spiritually? (John 6:57). Do you listen to the hunger pangs of your soul with the same concern as you listen to the hunger pangs of your stomach? Are you as obedient to the one desire as you are to the other? Does your prayer life reflect that belief? What do you really believe, anyway?

Jesus said, "It is written: 'Man does not live on bread alone, but on every *word* that comes from the mouth of God'" (Matthew 4:4, emphasis added). Do you believe that the words of God are crucial to your life?

> "The Spirit gives life; the flesh counts for nothing. The *words* I have spoken to you are spirit and they are life...."
> Simon Peter answered him, "Lord, to whom shall we go? You have the *words* of eternal life. We believe and know

that you are the Holy One of God." (John 6:63, 68–69,
emphasis added)

Our daily habit of Bible study reflects what we really believe about the words of God. What do we really believe about our Bibles?

Do You Still Believe?

The people asked Jesus, "What must we do to do the works God requires?" (John 6:28). If someone asked you that question, what would your reply be? Until studying this passage of scripture, my response would have been something along the lines of: "Well, you need to read your Bible, pray, come to church, repent of the sin in your life, learn to be more loving, share your faith and become a disciple of Jesus Christ." But, that is not what Jesus said: "Jesus answered, 'The work of God is this: to believe in the one he has sent'" (John 6:29).

For many of us, our first reaction to this response from Jesus is: "Come on, Jesus, you're being too easy on them! Tell them the real work. Tell them about discipleship and cross-bearing. Tell them about sacrifice and suffering for your name. Tell them about sharing your faith and dedicating yourself to making disciples the rest of your life. Tell them about the real work of being a disciple!"

But, as usual, our thinking is wrong and Jesus' thinking is right. Let's consider more carefully what Jesus is really saying here. The real work of God, the thing that takes the most effort, the most energy, the most work in the Christian life, is to believe! After you have become a disciple and have repented of all your sins, and then find you still have trouble with the toughest of them, do you still believe that you have the power to overcome sin? After you have prayed earnestly, sincerely and persistently about something you wanted and you didn't get it, do you still believe that God answers prayer? After you have poured your life into that person and he or she did well for a while, but now is right back where they started, or perhaps even worse, has become unfaithful, do you still believe that you can be successful in discipling others to maturity in Christ, and in seeking and saving the lost?

You want to talk about work? The real work of God is not the acts of obedience that we think are so hard, but rather it is putting our faith and trust in an unseen and unfathomable God who rarely behaves as we think he should or want him to.

It is hard to pray—not because it is so hard to discipline ourselves to get up in the morning and carry out our daily routine (there is some difficulty in that simple task, though many of us are committed to a regular workout regimen or other daily routine that requires the same self-discipline to carry out). But prayer is uniquely difficult because prayer takes faith. Throughout the Gospels, we see Jesus constantly trying to instill this kind of faith in his disciples:

> "Have faith in God," Jesus answered. "I tell you the truth, if anyone says to this mountain, 'Go, throw yourself into the sea,' and does not doubt in his heart but believes that what he says will happen, it will be done for him. Therefore I tell you, whatever you ask for in prayer, believe that you have received it, and it will be yours." (Mark 11:22–24)

This is why the words of Paul have always inspired me so much: "I urge you, brothers, by our Lord Jesus Christ and by the love of the Spirit, to join me in my struggle by praying to God for me" (Romans 15:30). Paul believed in prayer because Paul believed in the God of prayer! Paul knew he needed prayer because Paul knew he needed God. Paul believed in the power of intercessory prayer because he believed in the power and willingness of God to work in our lives. Paul reveals the deep faith that he has in this work of prayer by sincerely asking the Christians at Rome to join him in his struggle by praying to God for him.

Will We Believe?

Is prayer a struggle for you? You are not alone. It is a struggle for all of us. Perhaps the case could be made that genuine prayer is the greatest struggle in the Christian life. I don't know. But I know this: we must stop feeling like there is something wrong with us when we don't want to pray. We must not allow Satan to accuse us with thoughts of self-condemnation and self-doubt about this area of our lives. We must recognize that prayer is hard work. Watch how Paul puts it as he describes the prayer life of a disciple named Epaphras: "He is *always wrestling in prayer for you*, that you may stand firm in all the will of God, mature and fully assured. I vouch for him that he is *working hard for you* and for those at Laodicea and Hierapolis" (Colossians 4:12–13, emphasis added). Prayer is a wrestling match, (remember the story of Jacob wrestling with God in prayer, Genesis 32:24–30); wrestling is hard work!

If we are going to be successful prayer warriors, then we've got to be aggressive about going to the Scriptures for the faith that we need every day. We've got to allow scriptures like this one to fill our faith-tanks full: "May the God of hope fill you with all joy and peace as you trust in him, so that you may overflow with hope by the power of the Holy Spirit" (Romans 15:13). And then we will have the faith to go out and pray with passion, fervor and conviction. What is the work that God requires? The work of God is to believe!

In Luke 18, Jesus had been talking about prayer by telling the story of a persistent widow who was not getting the justice she deserved from an uncompassionate judge. But the woman won her case because she refused to give up. Jesus uses her as a picture of persistence; he urges us to relentlessly tug on God's sleeve as this woman does. And then Jesus ends the parable by wondering aloud: "However, when the Son of Man comes, will he find faith on the earth?" (Luke 18:8).

The question begs an answer. You and I had faith yesterday. Will we continue to have it today and tomorrow? Remember, the work of God is this: to believe!

Satan Attacks Our Faith

Nehemiah was moved by God to travel back to his homeland

and rebuild the walls of Jerusalem, which had been broken down for almost a century and a half, and had left the city vulnerable to attack (Nehemiah 1–2). But when Nehemiah got there, he soon found out that it would not be an easy task. A rival Samaritan official named Sanballat immediately made it his goal to vigorously oppose Nehemiah's project, as it posed a threat to his own political interests:

> When Sanballat heard that we were rebuilding the wall, he became angry and was greatly incensed. He ridiculed the Jews, and in the presence of his associates and the army of Samaria, he said, "What are those feeble Jews doing? Will they restore their wall? Will they offer sacrifices? Will they finish in a day? Can they bring the stones back to life from those heaps of rubble—burned as they are?" (Nehemiah 4:1–2)

If we look carefully, it is not hard to see Satan in this picture. Sanballat has become "angry and greatly incensed" because Nehemiah has undertaken to do the Lord's work and promote the welfare of God's people, so he "ridiculed the Jews" with critical questions that pointed out their weaknesses, inadequacies and past failures. Notice Satan's message: "It can't be done." This is a direct attack on Nehemiah's faith! And that is exactly what Satan says to us all the time. "What is this feeble Christian trying to accomplish? Will he really make a comeback in his life and be spiritually strong again? And how long will that take him? Does he really think that he can bring that heap of rubble back to life, burned out as it is?" Sound familiar? Satan has been barraging mankind with this sort of negative talk and slander for centuries. He is good at it, and he is not going to let up now!

The Importance of Faith

Satan attacks our faith because he knows how important our faith is to us. At the Last Supper, Jesus soberly told Simon Peter, "Simon, Simon, Satan has asked to sift you as wheat. But I have prayed for you, Simon, that your *faith* may not fail. And when you have turned back, strengthen your brothers" (Luke 22:31–32, emphasis added). Jesus knew that Peter would fall in his hour of weakness, but his prayer was that Peter would not abandon his faith altogether. Jesus prayed that Peter would hang on to his faith, because he knew that even if he fell into sin, if he still believed, then he could come back again and be restored. Notice Jesus says, "When you have turned back." Jesus never doubted that Peter would stay faithful even through this most difficult trial in his life. And he has that same belief in you and me today.

Jesus often talked about the crucial role of faith in those whom he healed. After a woman with a long-term illness broke through her doubts and fears long enough to touch Jesus' cloak and receive the healing she desired, Jesus turned to her and said, "Take heart, daughter, your faith has healed you" (Matthew 9:22). And after he healed two blind men who had been calling out for mercy to him on the street, Jesus told them, "According to your faith will it be done to you" (Matthew 9:29).

Consider this: what did Jesus challenge the apostles most about in the three years that he was with them? Was it their purity or their commitment? No, he challenged them most frequently on their lack of faith—because he knew their faith was the basis for everything else about them.

Jesus to apostles:

> "You of little faith, why are you so afraid?" (Matthew 8:26)

Jesus to Peter:

> "You of little faith, why did you doubt?" (Matthew 14:33)

Jesus to apostles:

> "You of little faith, why are you talking among yourselves about having no bread? Do you still not understand?" (Matthew 16:8)

> Then the disciples came to Jesus in private and asked, "Why couldn't we drive it out?"
>
> He replied, "Because you have so little faith. I tell you the truth, if you have faith as small as a mustard seed, you can say to this mountain, 'Move from here to there' and it will move. Nothing will be impossible for you." (Matthew 17:19–21)

If Jesus were to appear to you today and challenge you, what do you think he would bring up? Most likely, your lack of faith. Jesus knows that our faith is the basis for everything else he is trying to accomplish in our lives. Even love, while greater (1 Corinthians 13:13) is still dependent on faith: "The only thing that counts is faith expressing itself through love" (Galatians 5:6).

What do Satan and Jesus both know that many of us do not? That it all comes down to faith.

The Battle for Faith

Notice what the ground floor is in Peter's depiction of how we build our spiritual lives:

> For this very reason, make every effort to add to your *faith* goodness; and to goodness, knowledge; and to knowledge, self-control; and to self-control, perseverance; and to perseverance, godliness; and to godliness, brotherly kindness; and to brotherly kindness, love." (2 Peter 1:5–7, emphasis added)

Isaiah tells us: "The Sovereign Lord says, 'If you do not stand firm in your faith, you will not stand at all'" (Isaiah 7:9).

Have you ever noticed the pattern of faith leading to action found in the great "hall of faith" passage, Hebrews 11?

By faith, Abel offered a better sacrifice than Cain.

By faith, Noah built an ark.

By faith, Abraham when called to leave his home, obeyed and went.

By faith, Isaac blessed Jacob.

By faith, Moses chose to be mistreated along with the people of God rather than to enjoy the pleasures of sin for a short time.

By faith, the people passed through the Red Sea as on dry land.

By faith, the walls of Jericho fell, after the people had marched around them for seven days.

By faith, Rahab hid the spies.

By faith, Gideon, Barak, Samson, Jephthah, David, Samuel and the prophets:

> conquered kingdoms,
> administered justice,
> shut the mouths of lions,
> quenched the fury of the flames,
> escaped the edge of the sword,
> became powerful in battle and routed foreign armies.

The pattern is clear: faith leads to action! After the litany of names, the Bible simply says, "These were all commended for their *faith*" (Hebrews 11:39, emphasis added). They were not commended for their heroics, though they were heroes; they were not commended for their courage, though they were courageous; they were not commended for their military success, though they were successful. They were commended for their faith, because their faith is what enabled their courageous and heroic successes!

Abraham: A Model of Faith

> Against all hope, Abraham in hope believed and so became the father of many nations, just as it had been said to him, "So shall your offspring be." Without weakening in his faith, he faced the fact that his body was as good as dead—since he was about a hundred years old—and that Sarah's womb was also dead. Yet he did not waver through unbelief regarding the promise of God, but was strengthened in his faith and gave glory to God, being fully persuaded that God had power to do what he had promised. (Romans 4:18–21)

This is the kind of faith I want to have! "Against all hope, Abraham in hope believed" (v18). This is what comebacks are made of. When the chips are down and everyone's counting you out; when it's near the end of the game, and you're behind in the score; when nobody believes in you but your invisible God—that's the time to see what you're made of.

I love football, especially the playoffs. I will never forget the 1992 AFC Wildcard game between the Houston Oilers and the Buffalo Bills. Veteran Houston quarterback Warren Moon had been on target for four touchdown passes in the first half, and the Oilers were ahead 28–3 at halftime. Any hopes for a Buffalo comeback were apparently dashed when Oilers' safety Bubba McDowell returned an interception fifty-eight yards for another touchdown, making the score 35–3 early in the third quarter, and putting the Bills behind by thirty-two points. No team in the history of the NFL had ever come back to win after being behind by so many points. But at least one player on the field that day believed it could be done—backup Bills quarterback, Frank Reich.

This substitute quarterback, who was filling in for the injured Jim Kelly, began the unlikely comeback by leading his team on a fifty-yard touchdown drive. Then Buffalo kicker Steve Christie recovered his own onside kick, and quarterback Reich led them on another quick strike drive, scoring on a thirty-eight-yard touchdown pass. The Oilers went three and out, and another four-play touchdown drive put the Buffalo Bills back in the game, 35–24.

Sensing new life, the Buffalo defense came alive and intercepted Moon on his next series, setting up an eighteen-yard pass play from Reich to Andre Reed, making the score 35–31 late in the third quarter. After a back and forth stalemate for nearly fourteen minutes, the Bills finally broke through again, driving down the field seventy-four yards on seven plays for yet another touchdown, giving them the lead for the first time in the game, 38–35, with just under three minutes to play. But Moon rallied the Oilers for a last gasp effort and managed to score a last-second field goal, sending the game into overtime.

The Oilers won the overtime coin toss and elected to receive, but Bills defensive back Nate Odoms quickly intercepted a

Warren Moon pass to set the stage for Buffalo kicker Steve Christie to come in and kick the game-winning field goal, sending the Bills into the record books with the NFL's greatest comeback ever! Now, that's a comeback! But the Buffalo Bills couldn't have done it if a second-string quarterback hadn't believed, against all odds, that it could be done. Against all hope, one man believed—and it changed the outcome of the game.

What is the score in your game? It may be already in the second half with the clock ticking. The odds are against you and your opponent is fierce; but the game is not over yet. God has called your number and you are in the game. You run to the huddle and all your teammates are looking at you. They are worn and tired, battered and bruised, and they are looking to you to call the next play. It's gut-check time. It's time for faith. It's time for you to remember who you are, what your name is, and fulfill your destiny. Go ahead, look them in the eye, call the play, and go lead them to victory! You can do it—by faith!

A Lady of Faith

She was the last person anyone figured to end up being one of Jesus' very best friends. He was pure, she was impure; he was holy, she was unholy; he was a man of God, she was a woman of the streets. They say everyone has their demons to fight, but Mary Magdalene had been possessed by seven of them (Luke 8:2).[1]

We can only imagine how difficult it must have been for Mary to approach Jesus for healing. Imagine the courage it must have taken. She had to walk past the Pharisees with their condescending looks, the teachers of the law with their self-righteous attitudes, and even the other women who knew who and what she was—on her way to the One who she hoped would see past all of that and into the heart of a scared little girl who only wanted to start over again.

My good friend, Kim Pullen, has captured the essence of her task in the following song. Here are the lyrics:

Mary Magdalene's Song

I thought I'd become an expert
on the human eye.
I'd seen every look and glance and glare
when people'd pass me by.

They knew my occupation—
a lady of the night.
But I was not a victim.
I chose to live this life.

Eyes that cut, eyes that blame
Everyone was all the same.
How I wished someone would see
past the prostitute in me.

I didn't do it for the pleasure.
That may seem hard to understand.
I just wanted one man to see me
for the person that I am.

Eyes that pity, eyes that shame—
silently accusing with every name.
All eyes looked, but could never see
the lonely child inside of me.

Then a man—this man—looked at me,
eyes without lust and free of greed,
eyes of age yet rich with youth
that simply said, "I believe in you."

And like the leper that he chose to touch
"You're forgiven!" cleansed so much.
Changed from the butt of every slur—
I was now a woman, free and pure.

Eyes that sing, eyes that shout—
eyes that tell what life's really about.
This man was so much more than he seemed.
This man—my friend—gave me back my dream.

The Bible tells us that Mary Magdalene went on to become a devoted follower of Jesus and one of his very best friends. After repenting of her sinful lifestyle, she became one of the women who supported his ministry financially (Luke 8:2–3); she was one of the few who stayed close to Jesus throughout his crucifixion, comforting Jesus' mother at the foot of the cross (John 19:25); and she, along with two other women, went to the tomb with spices to anoint Jesus' body after his death, when they were met by an angel who announced Jesus' resurrection to them (Mark 16:1–7).

Perhaps most touching is the passage in Mark's gospel that records a very special moment that I am sure Mary Magdalene never forgot: "When Jesus rose early on the first day of the week, *he appeared first to Mary Magdalene*, out of whom he had driven seven demons" (Mark 16:9, emphasis added). Mary never forgot her Lord, and apparently her Lord never forgot her.

The Heart of a Champion

I will close this chapter with one more poem from Kim Pullen. It is one of my personal favorites. It describes the heart of Mary Magdalene, the heart of Abraham, and the heart of every disciple of Jesus who is determined by faith to cross that finish line some day.

The Heart of a Champion

It is my choice. It is my decision.

I determine who I will be and who I will follow.

No circumstance will alter my course.
No difficulty will block my path.

Though excruciating pain may slow me
and tears of disappointment blind me,
I will grope,
I will fight,
I will push myself to be all that God believes I can be.

And what carries me across the finish line,
will not be the muscle of strength
or the mind of knowledge,
it will be my heart,
the Heart of a Champion.

Standing on the Promises

Standing on the promises of Christ my King,
Through eternal ages let his praises ring.
"Glory in the highest!" I will shout and sing,
Standing on the promises of God.

Standing on the promises that cannot fail,
When the howling storms of doubt and fear assail.
By the living word of God I shall prevail;
Standing on the promises of God.

Standing on the promises of Christ, the Lord,
Bound to him eternally by love's strong cord.
Overcoming daily with the Spirit's sword,
Standing on the promises of God.

Standing on the promises, I cannot fall,
Listening every moment to the Spirit's call.
Resting in my Savior as my all in all;
Standing on the promises of God.

8

STANDING ON THE
PROMISES

The Promises of God

One of the most exciting topics in the entire Bible is "the promises of God." Just imagine: the most powerful, intelligent, loving and trustworthy Being in the universe has made specific promises to you and me about how he will bless our lives. He is a doting Father at his son or daughter's birthday party, a Prince in love at the beck and call of his betrothed, a King enamored with his special dinner guests, eager to give them a night they will never forget! God wants to lavish his gifts on us, shower us with his blessings and overwhelm us with his love. "'Test me in this,' says the LORD Almighty, 'and see if I will not throw open the floodgates of heaven and pour out so much blessing that you will not have room enough for it'" (Malachi 3:10). Wow! The gates of heaven being thrown open and God's blessings flooding into your living room—how does that sound? Does it sound too good to be true? Not when you consider the one who is saying it. God has always wanted to bless our lives richly. And he certainly has the resources and ability to do it!

In our last chapter we talked about the importance of faith to our spiritual lives—but faith in what? We need faith in God, for sure, but more specifically we need to place our faith in the character and promises of God.

> His divine power has given us everything we need for life
> and godliness through our knowledge of him who called
> us by his own glory and goodness. Through these he has
> given us his very great and precious promises, so that
> through them you may participate in the divine nature
> and escape the corruption in the world caused by evil
> desires. (2 Peter 1:3–4)

The character of God, specifically his qualities of glory and goodness according to this passage, are the basis of his promises. In other words, because God is so good and glorious, he has given us some great and precious promises. So our faith is first in his character—that we trust God because of who he is—and second in his promises, because we know that our good and glorious God would never lie to us. His promises are absolutely trustworthy. That makes God's promises "an anchor for the soul, firm and secure" (Hebrews 6:19).

Now watch how vital the promises of God are to our spiritual health: Peter teaches us that it is through them (God's promises) that we can actually "participate in the divine nature and escape the corruption in the world caused by evil desires" (v4). So, the promises of God are the tools that we use to tune up our spiritual engines. They will not do anything for us if they remain in the toolbox. But if we pick them up and learn how to use them properly, they will fix any problem this world can throw at us.

Another way of looking at it is that if we have been in a spiritual pit and faith is the belief that we can get out of the pit, then "the promises of God" is the rope that God throws us to grab hold of so that we can climb out. That is how God wants us to view and use his promises, as a rope to hang onto so that we can willfully climb out of whatever trap Satan has caused us to fall into. We can pull on them, one at a time, hand over hand, raising our bodies until we finally crawl out of the pit and get back on the road again with God.

As you can see, learning how to place our faith in the promises of God is standard equipment for every pilgrim along this spiritual journey. So, let's take some climbing lessons and figure out how to use this rope that God has thrown us.

Climbing Lessons

They say, "Give a man a fish, feed him for a day; teach a man to fish, feed him for a lifetime." I am so grateful to have been a disciple in the San Diego Church of Christ in the mid-1980s when Gordon Ferguson served as our lead evangelist. Gordon spent much time teaching us how to dig into the Bible for ourselves and mine the gems out of it. One of the lessons he taught us that made quite an impact on me was to read the Scriptures asking three questions of the text in order to bring it into sharper focus: One, is there a fact to believe here? Two, is there a promise to trust? And, three, is there a command to obey?

The concept is taken from Hebrews 11:6: "And without faith it is impossible to please God, because anyone who comes to him must believe that he exists and that he rewards those who earnestly seek him." In other words, according to this verse, faith that pleases God

1. Must believe (that he exists)
2. Must trust (that he rewards)
3. Must obey (his command to earnestly seek him)

A faithful response to scripture will always include these three elements: belief, trust and obedience.

Go ahead; try this method out for yourself the next time you are reading your Bible. Ask yourself: "Is there a fact to believe here? Is there a promise to trust? Is there a command to obey?" You will find the Scriptures really applying to your life when you read them this way.

Of course when you start looking for promises to trust in God's word, you'll soon find that they are all over the Bible! God has not been stingy in doling out his promises. He has liberally scattered them throughout the pages of his inspired word to make it easy for you to pick them up and use them.

Eight Promises of God

Obviously it would be impossible for me to present to you all of the promises of God in this chapter (and that would take all the fun out of your own search!). So, I have selected just a few promises that have helped me to climb out of the traps of Satan through the years and stay on course with God. I hope you will find them equally useful.

Whenever you pray, I will answer you.

> "Ask and it will be given to you; seek and you will find; knock and the door will be opened to you. For everyone who asks receives; he who seeks finds; and to him who knocks, the door will be opened.
> "Which of you, if his son asks for bread, will give him a stone? Or if he asks for a fish, will give him a snake? If you, then, though you are evil, know how to give good gifts to your children, how much more will your Father in heaven give good gifts to those who ask him!" (Matthew 7:7–11)

This is a very precious promise to me because I have hung on to it many times through the years. Jesus doesn't say, "If you're good enough, I'll answer your prayers." He says, "*Everyone* who asks receives" (v8). I like that because it includes me—even on my bad days. In fact, that is when he wants to hear from me the most.

I like the definitive nature of the promise Jesus is making as well. He doesn't say, "Ask and it *may* be given to you; seek and you *may* find; knock and the door *may* be opened to you." No! Jesus (who can be thoroughly trusted) says emphatically and authoritatively, "Ask and it *will* be given to you; seek and you *will* find; knock and the door *will* be opened to you" (v7, emphasis added). Make no mistake about it: if you ask, you will receive; if you seek, you will find; and if you knock, the door will be opened to you! Sort of makes you want to start asking doesn't it? That's the point.

Here are a few more mouthwatering prayer promises:

> "And I will do whatever you ask in my name, so that the

> Son may bring glory to the Father. You may ask me for anything in my name, and I will do it." (John 14:13–14)
>
> This is the confidence we have in approaching God: that if we ask anything according to his will, he hears us. And if we know that he hears us—whatever we ask—we know that we have what we asked of him. (1 John 5:14–15)
>
> "If you believe, you will receive whatever you ask for in prayer." (Matthew 21:22)

Someone once said that when we get to heaven and think back on our time here on earth, the most surprising thing to us will be how little we prayed. With promises like this written to us, it is amazing we don't pray more than we do. Let's grab hold of these promises on prayer and let God hoist us up to another level.

Give me your anxieties, and I will give you peace.

> Do not be anxious about anything, but in everything, by prayer and petition, with thanksgiving, present your requests to God. And the peace of God, which transcends all understanding, will guard your hearts and your minds in Christ Jesus. (Philippians 4:6–7)

There is that authoritative word "will" again: "…will guard your hearts and minds in Christ Jesus" (v7). I don't know how many times I have reached up and grabbed hold of that word in this verse and hung on for dear life, like a mountain climber hanging onto a rock protruding out of the ledge. None of us has inner peace without God. The irony is that inner peace must come from an external source. And there is no other external source out there that can give peace like God can. His peace isn't the temporary relief of a drug, but a spiritual peace that enters into our souls like a healing vapor from heaven to soothe our sore hearts and ease our weary minds.

Of course there are also some prerequisite commands to obey in this passage. Verse 6 instructs us to "not be anxious about anything, but in everything, by prayer and petition, with thanksgiving, present [our] requests to God." That is a small price to pay for peace. I remember hearing many years ago that a famous rock-and-roll star once offered a million dollars to the person that could give him genuine peace for just one hour! That is how valuable peace is to most of us. I know it's that valuable to me. That is why I am glad I became a Christian and somebody showed me this verse. Now all I have to do is keep putting it into practice so I can keep receiving the peace of God that "transcends all understanding."

How about you—need any peace in your life? Here are a few more scriptures to consider:

> Cast all your anxiety on him because he cares for you. (1 Peter 5:7)

> "Peace I leave with you; my peace I give you. I do not give to you as the world gives. Do not let your hearts be troubled and do not be afraid." (John 14:27)

> "Come to me, all you who are weary and burdened, and I will give you rest. Take my yoke upon you and learn from me, for I am gentle and humble in heart, and you will find rest for your souls. For my yoke is easy and my burden is light." (Matthew 11:28–30)

> My soul finds rest in God alone;
>   my salvation comes from him.
> He alone is my rock and my salvation;
>   he is my fortress, I will never be shaken.
> (Psalm 62:1–2)

That last one (Psalm 62:1–2) kept me sane through college. I felt so confused and insecure after all the partying I had done as a non-Christian. My brain was unclear and my heart was polluted. But when someone introduced me to the Bible, God directed me to this verse. I used to read it every night to comfort my troubled mind. Soon I became a Christian, and God's peace entered my heart through his Holy Spirit (Galatians 5:22); the guilt melted away and the insecurities slowly dissipated. The promises in this verse have proven to be true in my life. My soul looked for rest in so many places, but found it in God alone; my salvation comes from him. He is my rock, my fortress; I can no longer be shaken. I hope God will use this verse to bring you peace as well.

When you're afraid, I'll be there for you.

> So do not fear, for I am with you;
>   do not be dismayed, for I am your God.
> I will strengthen you and help you;
>   I will uphold you with my righteous right hand.
> (Isaiah 41:10)

When my children were younger, they would occasionally come into our bedroom at night because they were scared. After they had snuggled beside us, they were so secure that they fell right to sleep. Nothing had changed for them except that before they were alone in their room—now they were with their parents. That made all the difference; everything was going to be all right.

Aren't we the same way with our heavenly Father? We just want to know that he is there for us—watching over us, taking care of us and protecting us. And you know what? I think he likes it when we need him that way, just like we parents like feeling needed by our own kids. So, go ahead, curl up beside him and snuggle; or grab hold of his hand as you walk along the way. It will make you feel better, and he will love it more than you can possibly imagine. Here are a few more loops of promise-rope to hang on to:

> The LORD is my light and my salvation—
>   whom shall I fear?
> The LORD is the stronghold of my life—
>   of whom shall I be afraid?
> Though an army besiege me,
>   my heart will not fear;
> though war break out against me,
>   even then will I be confident. (Psalm 27:1, 3)

> The LORD is with me; I will not be afraid.
>   What can man do to me?
> The LORD is with me; he is my helper.
>   I will look in triumph on my enemies. (Psalm 118:6–7)

> "Have I not commanded you? Be strong and coura-
> geous. Do not be terrified; do not be discouraged, for
> the LORD your God will be with you wherever you go."
> (Joshua 1:9)

I will get you through your trials, and you'll be better for them.

> No temptation has seized you except what is common to
> man. And God is faithful; he will not let you be tempted
> beyond what you can bear. But when you are tempted,
> he will also provide a way out so that you can stand up
> under it. (1 Corinthians 10:13)

> Consider it pure joy, my brothers, whenever you face tri-
> als of many kinds, because you know that the testing of
> your faith develops perseverance. Perseverance must fin-
> ish its work so that you may be mature and complete,
> not lacking anything. (James 1:2–4)

These two verses have gotten me through so many trials! The first one tells me that God is in control of everything that I am subjected to, even the trials and temptations that I face. He will not let me face anything that I can't handle, as long as I rely on his power. That is encouraging. The second verse tells me why he allows anything bad in my life at all—it is because I need those things to refine my character and become more like Jesus.

Like in a heavy-weight boxing match, there are short jabs in life. Then there are the big roundhouse punches that can catch us off guard and knock us to the canvas. Both are under the sovereign control of God. But it is the knock-out punches that we have to especially be on our guard against. They will come, to be sure. But we have got to rely enough on the promises of God in Scripture to be able to get back up before the referee counts to ten.

Another verse that has helped me greatly to get back up when I have been knocked down by life is Romans 8:28–30:

> And we know that in all things God works for the good
> of those who love him, who have been called according
> to his purpose. For those God foreknew he also predes-
> tined to be conformed to the likeness of his Son, that he

might be the firstborn among many brothers. And those he predestined, he also called; those he called, he also justified; those he justified, he also glorified.

These verses promise that God will get me through whatever trial I am facing, and they also give an explanation for why I am facing the trial: so I can be "conformed to the likeness of his Son" (v29). Knowing that "in all things God works for the good of those who love him" (v28) encourages us because we know that even though bad things may happen to us, God will bring good things out of them. We are not promised that life will be easy. But we are promised that God will take care of us through our trials and bring good out of bad. That is a pretty good promise—one that can help us get through just about anything.

Put me first, and I'll take care of you financially.

Remember this: Whoever sows sparingly *will* also reap sparingly, and whoever sows generously *will* also reap generously. Each man should give what he has decided in his heart to give, not reluctantly or under compulsion, for God loves a cheerful giver. And God is able to make all grace abound to you, so that in all things at all times, having all that you need, you *will* abound in every good work...

Now he who supplies seed to the sower and bread for food *will* also supply and increase your store of seed and *will* enlarge the harvest of your righteousness. You will be made rich in every way so that you can be generous on every occasion, and through us your generosity *will* result in thanksgiving to God. (2 Corinthians 9:6–8, 10–11, emphasis added)

Once again we see the definitive word "will" used several times. Watch how these promises come alive when we emphasize what God says he will do for us:

- Whoever sows sparingly will also reap sparingly.
- Whoever sows generously will also reap generously.
- God is able to make all grace abound to you, so that in all things at all times, having all that you need, you will abound in every good work.
- Now he who supplies seed to the sower and bread for food will

also supply and increase your store of seed and will enlarge the harvest of your righteousness.
- You will be made rich in every way.
- Your generosity will result in thanksgiving to God.

Don't you just love the promises of God? I mean, you can take this one to the bank! God clearly is promising us that if we do our part to support his work financially, then he will make sure we are taken care of financially as well, and our generosity will result in thanksgiving to God—that makes good sense all the way around!

Don't worry, no one is getting away with anything; I'm in control.

> Do not fret because of evil men
> or be envious of those who do wrong;
> for like the grass they will soon wither,
> like green plants they will soon die away.
> Be still before the LORD and wait patiently for him;
> do not fret when men succeed in their ways,
> when they carry out their wicked schemes.
> Refrain from anger and turn from wrath;
> do not fret—it leads only to evil.
> For evil men will be cut off,
> but those who hope in the LORD will inherit the land.
> A little while, and the wicked will be no more;
> though you look for them, they will not be found.
> But the meek will inherit the land
> and enjoy great peace. (Psalm 37:1–2, 7–11)

There is not much that can irritate us, anger us and rile us more than injustice. Just think of how many movies play on the theme of revenge—it is a powerful emotion. Our hero is unjustly treated, perhaps his wife and children are mistreated, or he himself is mistreated or unjustly accused, and he is nobly patient throughout the beginning of the movie. Then the bad guys are pushing and pushing the audience's buttons, getting us more and more angry at the injustice on the screen, until finally our hero can stand no more and he spends the rest of the movie getting back at the bad guys, to the great delight of the movie audience. Sound familiar? Of course it does, it has been a formula for success in the movie industry for years.

That is why Jesus' example and teaching on this subject are so radical. Jesus taught us to turn the other cheek and give our cloak to the one who is already unjustly taking our tunic (Matthew 5:38–42). That is hardly a formula for a successful Hollywood screenplay!

I know for me, not retaliating against those whom I have felt mistreated by is one of the hardest things to do as a Christian. I have spent many anguished hours in prayer through the years, as well as venting my feelings with my wife and then hearing her remind me to respond as Jesus would in the situation (praise God for a spiritual wife!).

But it dawned on me a few years ago when I was studying this out for a friend, that God does not expect us to simply act like nothing happened when in fact it has. He understands that injustice causes pain and has provided for our healing by assuring us that the perpetrator will not get away with anything; in fact he will be punished some day—maybe in this life, or maybe in the next. Either way, there is a sense of justice and vindication that God wants to give us to help heal our hurts. Don't get me wrong, we need to completely forgive any and all who mistreat us every time we are wronged and not retaliate in any way against them. But God also wants us to know that the universe is a just place and nobody is going to get away with anything. Consider the following passages:

> Do not take revenge, my friends, but leave room for God's wrath, for it is written: "It is mine to avenge; I will repay," says the Lord. (Romans 12:19)

> "It is mine to avenge; I will repay.
>   In due time their foot will slip;
> their day of disaster is near
>   and their doom rushes upon them."
> (Deuteronomy 32:35)

> Contend, O Lord, with those who contend with me;
>   fight against those who fight against me.
> Take up shield and buckler;

> arise and come to my aid.
> Brandish spear and javelin
>   against those who pursue me.
> Say to my soul,
>   "I am your salvation."
> Then my soul will rejoice in the LORD
>   and delight in his salvation.
> My whole being will exclaim,
>   "Who is like you, O LORD?
> You rescue the poor from those too strong for them,
>   the poor and needy from those who rob them."
> Vindicate me in your righteousness, O LORD my God;
>   do not let them gloat over me.
> (Psalm 35:1–3, 9–10, 24)

There is something very comforting about knowing our God will not allow injustice to go unpunished, but will vindicate us eventually. The scripture that really nails it down for me is one about how Jesus handled his own unjust crucifixion: "When they hurled their insults at him, he did not retaliate; when he suffered, he made no threats. Instead, *he entrusted himself to him who judges justly*" (1 Peter 2:23, emphasis added). There is the key: we need to entrust ourselves to him who judges justly. God promises us that he is still in control; no one is getting away with anything.

I promise you that my way works best.

> Peter said to him, "We have left everything to follow you!"
> "I tell you the truth," Jesus replied, "no one who has left home or brothers or sisters or mother or father or children or fields for me and the gospel will fail to receive a hundred times as much in this present age (homes, brothers, sisters, mothers, children and fields—and with them, persecutions) and in the age to come, eternal life. But many who are first will be last, and the last first." (Mark 10:28–31)

Peter had a question for Jesus. In essence he said, "We've left home, family, friends and our occupations to follow you. Are you sure this is worth it?" Jesus didn't skip a beat. I imagine him looking straight at Peter and explaining to his dear friend with deep conviction, "The life I give you is a hundred times better than anything you left; stick with it and you will find this to be true."

It just doesn't make sense that the Christian life would be less fulfilling than a life without God, now does it? Don't you think the one who created the heart knows how to fill it? Don't you think "the author of life" (Acts 3:15) knows a thing or two about how it is best lived? Jesus said, "I have come that they may have life, and have it to the full" (John 10:10). Real life comes from the source of life (John 1:4), the creator of life (John 1:3), the giver of life (John 5:21, 40), the bread of life (John 6:35), the light of life (John 8:12), the resurrection and the life (John 11:25), the way, the truth and the life (John 14:6)—Jesus Christ. Jesus knows about life. We can trust that following him will always lead to the very best lifestyle available.

Some of us have gotten burned-out on the Christian life. But I submit to you that the problem is not with the Christian life, but with perhaps a misinterpretation or misapplication of it. God's word is unchanging, but God's church is constantly changing to try and align itself more and more with the unchanging word of God. The same process is true for each of us as individuals. We are trying through trial and error to remain close to God and to do his will. I urge you, do not give up on the Christian life—it works.

I guarantee you that heaven will be worth it!

> Therefore we do not lose heart. Though outwardly we are wasting away, yet inwardly we are being renewed day by day. For our light and momentary troubles are achieving for us an eternal glory that far outweighs them all. So we fix our eyes not on what is seen, but on what is unseen. For what is seen is temporary, but what is unseen is eternal. (2 Corinthians 4:16–18)

I am not sure any of us would characterize our troubles as "light and momentary." But maybe that is because we don't have the same eternal perspective that God has. We have been looking at the promises of God in this chapter and have seen that God is absolutely trustworthy when he has spoken to us about things we can see. Considering his flawless track-record, doesn't it make sense to trust him for the things that we can't see? God says that compared to our earthly troubles, heaven will be "an eternal glory that far outweighs them all." I don't know about you, but I can't wait to get to heaven! Whatever trials we have had to endure here on earth, one thing I know for sure: heaven will be totally worth it! (Read more about heaven in chapter 10.)

All I Ask of You

My wife's favorite theatre show is *Phantom of the Opera*. When you walk into the auditorium, the staging is so well done that you think you have entered into another world. Then the music starts, and it is so magnificent that you feel like it is transporting you to that other world. It is a passionate love story filled with mystery and intrigue, but there is a particular song that is so beautiful that it seems to enter a place in our hearts that few songs ever find their way into. I offer it here as a song that perhaps captures a little bit of the passionate love our God has for us, and we have for him. Let it sweep you away as you think about God serenading you with "his very great and precious promises" in the part of Raoul, and respond in your heart to God in the part of Christine.

All I Ask of You

(Raoul)
No more talk of darkness—
forget these wide-eyed fears.
I'm here;
nothing can harm you.
My words will warm and calm you.

Let me be your freedom.
Let daylight dry your tears.
I'm here;
with you, beside you,

to guard you and to guide you…

(Christine)
Say you love me every waking moment.
Turn my head with talk of summertime.
Say you need me with you now and always.
Promise me that all you say is true—
That's all I ask of you…

(Raoul)
Let me be your shelter.
Let me be your light.
You're safe—
no one will find you;
your fears are far behind you…

(Christine)
All I want is freedom—
a world with no more night;
and you,
always beside me,
to hold me and to hide me…

(Raoul)
Then say you'll share with me one love, one lifetime.
Let me lead you from your solitude.
Say you need me with you, here beside you.
Anywhere you go, let me go too—
that's all I ask of you…

(Christine)
Say you'll share with me one love, one lifetime.
Say the word and I will follow you.
Share each day with me, each night, each morning.
Say you love me…

(Raoul)
You know I do…

(Both)
  Love me—that's all I ask of you…[1]

Just Tell Me What to Do

I won't tell you what to do
but I'll show you who to follow
so your lives will be fulfilled
and your souls no longer hollow.

Jesus gives us life
and fills our days with wonder!
But man gives only rules
that tear our hearts asunder.

"Return to little children"
is what Jesus had to say.
Live from your hearts—
that's the better way!

But men want rules to follow
like Pharisees of long ago,
so we don't have to think and feel—
just put it in cruise control.

"Just tell me what to do.
I like it better that way.
Don't ask me to follow my heart.
My heart has led me astray."

But with visions of Jesus in mind
it can be different this time.
Just set your hearts above
and the path will surely shine!

Jesus said, "Follow me,
and we'll teach others to follow."
But put the cart before the horse,
and religion will soon be hollow.

Abundant life awaits
all those who live from their hearts!
It's harder to do, for sure—
but that's when the Spirit starts!

Look to Jesus today!
Let go the rules of men.
Come back to the heart of God,
and let's start over again!

I won't tell you what to do,
but I'll show you who to follow
so your lives will be fulfilled
and your souls no longer hollow.

—*Jeff Chacon*

9

WHERE DREAMS GROW

Motivating Properly

Dreams grow best in the atmosphere of proper, Biblical motivation. What are the motivations that the Bible uses? There are many, including these: the fear of the Lord, the command to obey God, the gratitude for God's incredible mercy and grace, the sacrificial and unconditional love of God, the genuine desire to love our fellow man, the sense of duty and responsibility to carry out our mission, the desire to please God, the desire for heavenly reward, the joy and fulfillment of the Christian lifestyle, the personal satisfaction of simply knowing that we are doing what is right, and many, many more exciting motivations that are woven throughout the fabric of God's inspired word. In fact, an invigorating personal Bible study would be to go through the Scriptures and highlight all the different motivations you can find. That is a Bible study that is guaranteed to fire you up! Let's look at just a few of the primary motivations that God uses in Scripture.

Faith, Hope and Love

> We continually remember before our God and Father your *work produced by faith*, your *labor prompted by love*, and your *endurance inspired by hope* in our Lord Jesus Christ. (1 Thessalonians 1:3, emphasis added)

Some of us have sought to motivate others and ourselves by

emphasizing the need to "work," "labor" and "endure" in God's kingdom. But the Holy Spirit says that these three activities are the result of three other things: "faith," "love" and "hope." These are the seeds that we are to plant in order to harvest the result of work, labor and endurance, respectively. We must plant these motivational seeds of faith, love and hope in our hearts and water them constantly, trusting God to produce the results of work, labor and endurance in our lives and ministries, instead of trying to muster them artificially.

Simply commanding people to work for God may have short-term results, but eventually people will burn out if they don't have deeper motivation. The wise leader understands that God's word is a seed (Mark 4:14) that must be planted in the hearts of men in order to produce a crop (Mark 4:20). It is living and active (Hebrews 4:12) and grows like a seed in the soil of our hearts, though we do not know how (Mark 4:26–27). It is our job to plant and water the seed of God's word, while it is God's role to make it grow (1 Corinthians 3:6–7).

If we are to restore New Testament Christianity, then we must restore New Testament motivation. What worked then will work now, since the Bible is still relevant today. The Biblical leader instills faith in people, and they respond by working for God; he keeps God's love before them, and they are prompted to labor for God; he inspires them to hope, and they endure to the end because they know that it is worth it. These are long-term motivations that will sustain us throughout our lives.

The apostle Paul singled out these same three motivations in his first letter to the Corinthians: "And now these three remain: faith, hope and love. But the greatest of these is love" (1 Corinthians 13:13). What the Bible emphasizes, we too should emphasize. The fifth chapter of 2 Corinthians is one of the most inspiring chapters in the entire Bible and will be the basis of the next six motivations we discuss.

The Hope of Heaven

Paul begins by writing about heaven and then verbalizes something he feels strongly: "I would prefer to be away from the body and at home with the Lord" (2 Corinthians 5:8). Deep down, don't we all just want to go home and be with the Lord? I am reminded of the famous scene from Steven Spielberg's classic science fiction movie, *E.T. the Extra-Terrestrial*. The little lost and loveable alien is trying to communicate his homesickness to the earth boy who has befriended him, so he points to a telephone and says, "E.T. phone home." Don't we have that same desire deep down inside us as well? God has "set eternity in the hearts of men" (Ecclesiastes 3:11) as a sort of homing device to lead us home—to heaven where we belong.

The Holy Spirit actually directs us specifically to encourage each other with the hope of heaven:

> For the Lord himself will come down from heaven, with a loud command, with the voice of the archangel and with the trumpet call of God, and the dead in Christ will rise first. After that, we who are still alive and are left will be caught up together with them in the clouds to meet the Lord in the air. *And so we will be with the Lord forever. Therefore encourage each other with these words.* (1 Thessalonians 4:16–18, emphasis added)

This verse sure encourages me! I'll bet it encourages you too, and that is why God directs us to remind each other of it—to encourage us to persevere because of the hope of heaven. I will share more about heaven in chapter 10, which is dedicated solely to a discussion of this out-of-this-world promise of God. However, I wanted to mention it here because it is crucial that we view going to heaven as a valid motivation to love and obey God.

The Desire to Please God

Paul goes on to reveal another precious motivation in 2 Corinthians 5: "So we make it our goal to please him" (v9). Did you ever notice how natural it is for most of us to be people-pleasers? There are few people who genuinely don't care at all what other people think of them. That is because God has made us to want to please him—we just seem to substitute pleasing other people with pleasing God. Replacing our sinful desire to live for the praise of men with the correct desire to live for the praise of God is easier said than done:

> Yet at the same time many even among the leaders believed in him. But because of the Pharisees they would not confess their faith for fear they would be put out of the synagogue; for they loved praise from men more than praise from God. (John 12:42–43)

Yet as difficult as this task is, many of us have made that transition to a large extent, enduring persecution from perhaps even family and friends because of our faith, as Jesus said would happen (Matthew 10: 17–39). Why have we been willing to do that? Because even though it is very uncomfortable and often extremely difficult and painful to take an unpopular stand, we have found that there is simply nothing more satisfying than pleasing Almighty God! A good night's sleep and an easy smile in the morning are just two of the many rewards of pleasing God. It is inexplicably satisfying.

In addition, those who seek to please God above men will also excel in other areas of their lives: "Whatever you do, work at it with all your heart, as working for the Lord, not for men, since you know that you will receive an inheritance from the Lord as a reward. It is the Lord Christ you are serving" (Colossians 3:23–24). They excel because they are not out to do the minimum required, but the maximum possible; they are seeking to please an invisible God who sees all that they do in secret and rewards them accordingly (Matthew 6:6). So they tend to excel in life (work, school, relationships) and life tends to go better for them, both because of God's blessings and because of the natural rewards of excellence.

The Fear of Punishment

The next verse in 2 Corinthians 5 brings up a different motivation: "For we must all appear before the judgment seat of Christ, that each one may receive what is due him for the things done while in the body, whether good or bad" (v10). As the carrot is a valuable motivator, so is the stick.

At the end of the book of Ecclesiastes, the teacher who has searched his whole life for meaning, summarizes his findings with the following statement:

> Now all has been heard;
>   here is the conclusion of the matter:
> Fear God and keep his commandments,
>   for this is the whole duty of man.
> For God will bring every deed into judgment,
>   including every hidden thing,
>   whether it is good or evil. (Ecclesiastes 12:13–14)

I don't know about you, but that motivates me. I am not noble-hearted enough to consistently do what is right simply because it is the right thing to do. But knowing that I will meet my Maker and he will hold me accountable for the choices I made in my life helps me to do what is right. Praise God for this motivation in God's word!

Passages like these make me a better person:

> Nothing in all creation is hidden from God's sight. Everything is uncovered and laid bare before the eyes of him to whom we must give account. (Hebrews 4:13)

> This will take place on the day when God will judge men's secrets through Jesus Christ, as my gospel declares. (Romans 2:16)

> So then, each of us will give an account of himself to God. (Romans 14:12)

> He will bring to light what is hidden in darkness and will expose the motives of men's hearts. At that time each will receive his praise from God. (1 Corinthians 4:5)

> "The Lord will judge his people." It is a dreadful thing to

> fall into the hands of the living God. (Hebrews 10:30–31)
>
> Speak and act as those who are going to be judged by the law that gives freedom. (James 2:12)
>
> Not many of you should presume to be teachers, my brothers, because you know that we who teach will be judged more strictly. (James 3:1)
>
> Since you call on a Father who judges each man's work impartially, live your lives as strangers here in reverent fear. (1 Peter 1:17)

Some may say, "But I thought God wanted us to love him, not fear him." Actually our fear of God does not contradict our love for him. In fact, the fear of God helps us to love him better. Consider this illuminating scripture from the book of Exodus:

> When the people saw the thunder and lightning and heard the trumpet and saw the mountain in smoke, they trembled with fear. They stayed at a distance and said to Moses, "Speak to us yourself and we will listen. But do not have God speak to us or we will die."
> Moses said to the people, "Do not be afraid. God has come to test you, so that the fear of God will be with you to keep you from sinning." (Exodus 20:18–21)

Moses says, "Do not be afraid." We are not to fear that God is haphazard or capricious. He is not going to lose his temper with us and fly off the handle into a fit of rage like perhaps someone did with us when we were growing up, because that would be a sin and to sin is not the character of God. But we are to fear his righteous judgments against our sin, which motivates us not to sin: "…so that the fear of God will be with you to keep you from sinning" (v21).

God showed the people his awesome power that day in order to say in effect, "I am fully capable of enforcing these commandments I am giving you today." It is analogous perhaps to a loving father who must lay down the rules of the house with his children. In love, he wants them to understand that he is willing and able to enforce the rules he lays down for them. Should they fear him? Well, yes, they should fear the consequences of what will happen to them if they break the rules of the house that the father must enforce. But no, there is no reason to fear that he is going to be unfair, unkind or unreasonable in his application of those household rules because he is their loving father. And that is how God is with us—he inspires the right kind of fear and love in our hearts for him.

Noah understood this. The Bible records that he "in holy fear built an ark to save his family" (Hebrews 11:7). Maybe "holy fear" is the best way to say it. It is not the terror of one who rules with an iron fist, but it is the holy fear of one who governs justly and righteously.

Revelation 20 is a dramatic depiction of Judgment Day. I love this passage of scripture because it plays like a movie in my mind's eye and gives me a clear and sober picture of what that day will really be like:

> Then I saw a great white throne and him who was seated on it. Earth and sky fled from his presence, and there was no place for them. And I saw the dead, great and small, standing before the throne, and books were opened. Another book was opened, which is the book of life. The dead were judged according to what they had done as recorded in the books. The sea gave up the dead that were in it, and death and Hades gave up the dead that were in them, and each person was judged according to what he had done. Then death and Hades were thrown into the lake of fire. The lake of fire is the second death. If anyone's name was not found written in the book of life, he was thrown into the lake of fire. (Revelation 20:11–15)

I know I don't want to be thrown into the lake of fire—and I doubt you do either. That is a Biblical motivation to live for God!

Our Love for Others

The next verse in 2 Corinthians 5 naturally segues into

another powerful motivation—our love for others.

> Since, then, we know what it is to fear the Lord, we try
> to persuade men. (2 Corinthians 5:11)

After I became a Christian, nobody had to tell me to share my faith with my family. I did it because I loved them. I did it because I wanted them to have what I had and to find what I had found. I did it because I knew where they were spiritually, and didn't want to leave them behind. I did it because I had come to understand the judgment that they would face, and wanted desperately to prepare them for it.

In the story of the rich man and Lazarus, Jesus tells about a man who dies and goes to hell, and then suddenly gets real evangelistic about his family members who are still alive: "He answered, 'Then I beg you, father, send Lazarus to my father's house, for I have five brothers. Let him warn them, so that they will not also come to this place of torment'" (Luke 16:27–28). He learned to fear the Lord, and it moved him to try and persuade others. But it was too late for him to share with his family; he was already dead. It is not too late for us; we can still tell our family and loved ones about "sin and righteousness and judgment to come" (John 16:8). And it is our love for them that will motivate us to do it.

The Love of Christ

But the message that burns on our hearts to tell other people is not just about sin, righteousness and the judgment to come; it is equally about grace, mercy and the forgiveness of sins. Specifically it is about the magnificent heart of love that provides us with these things—the love of Christ!

> For Christ's love compels us, because we are convinced
> that one died for all, and therefore all died. And he died
> for all, that those who live should no longer live for them-
> selves but for him who died for them and was raised
> again. (2 Corinthians 5:14–15)

I love this scripture! I love that I am "compelled" by Christ's love! I love the fact that Jesus died on the cross for me—it makes me want to live my life for God.

There are many different motivations in the Christian life, and we must not neglect any of them, but the highest motivation must surely be the love of God for us through Jesus Christ. Watch how it motivates us according to the following scriptures:

> But by the grace of God I am what I am, and his grace to me was not without effect. No, I worked harder than all of them—yet not I, but the grace of God that was with me. (1 Corinthians 15:10)

> I have been crucified with Christ and I no longer live, but Christ lives in me. The life I live in the body, I live by faith in the Son of God, *who loved me and gave himself for me*. (Galatians 2:20, emphasis added)

> Therefore, I urge you, brothers, *in view of God's mercy*, to offer your bodies as living sacrifices, holy and pleasing to God—this is your spiritual act of worship. (Romans 12:1, emphasis added)

> At one time we too were foolish, disobedient, deceived and enslaved by all kinds of passions and pleasures. We lived in malice and envy, being hated and hating one another. But when the kindness and love of God our Savior appeared, he saved us, not because of righteous things we had done, but because of his mercy. He saved us through the washing of rebirth and renewal by the Holy Spirit, whom he poured out on us generously through Jesus Christ our Savior, so that, having been justified by his grace, we might become heirs having the hope of eternal life. This is a trustworthy saying. And I want you to stress these things, so that those who have trusted in God may be careful to devote themselves to doing what is good. These things are excellent and profitable for everyone. (Titus 3:3–8)

> This is how God showed his love among us: He sent his one and only Son into the world that we might live through him. This is love: not that we loved God, but that he loved us and sent his Son as an atoning sacrifice for

our sins. Dear friends, since God so loved us, we also ought to love one another. (1 John 4:10–11)

We love because he first loved us. (1 John 4:19)

God's love is the wind in our sails. Many times if we find ourselves stalled, it is because our sails are down and our boat is adrift, unable to gain any benefit from the wind. So, we've got to raise our sails again and catch hold of the wind of God's Spirit that is forever blowing. Don't let Satan take the wind out of your sails—focus on the love of God, and let him carry you away with the winds of his love.

On a Mission from God

There are few things more exciting in life than knowing you are on a mission from God. The adventure, excitement and thrill of it all give us the sense that life is worth living and the new day worth looking forward to. The One who created us and knows that we need a mission to fulfill in life has provided us with a better role than any Hollywood producer could ever come up with: we get to help God save the world!

All this is from God, who reconciled us to himself through Christ and gave us the ministry of reconciliation: that God was reconciling the world to himself in Christ, not counting men's sins against them. And he has committed to us the message of reconciliation. We are therefore Christ's ambassadors, as though God were making his appeal through us. We implore you on Christ's behalf: Be reconciled to God. (2 Corinthians 5:18–20)

Paul understood and relished his role as "Christ's ambassador" (v20). Look how he refers to himself in the following verses:

Unlike so many, we do not peddle the word of God for profit. On the contrary, in Christ we speak before God with sincerity, *like men sent from God*. (2 Corinthians 2:17, emphasis added)

As *God's fellow workers* we urge you not to receive God's grace in vain. (2 Corinthians 6:1, emphasis added)

> Paul, an apostle—*sent not from men nor by man, but by Jesus Christ and God the Father*, who raised him from the dead. (Galatians 1:1, emphasis added)

> We speak as *men approved by God to be entrusted with the gospel.* (1 Thessalonians 2:4, emphasis added)

Paul was excited about the role God had called him to play in the screenplay of life, and we have every reason to be so as well, since we too are called to be "Christ's ambassadors," "men sent from God," "God's fellow workers," and "men approved by God to be entrusted with the gospel." It is more than just a great role; it is a call to our destiny. It is a father whispering his dreams of the future in the ear of his son or daughter—and they spark a desire inside of us to become all that God envisions us to be!

Motivated by Jesus

There are so many other motivations we could talk about, but I want to close this chapter by directing your attention to one that is so obvious that it is easily missed. It is the simple and yet profound motivation of the person of Jesus Christ himself. Consider the following verses:

> "Just as Moses lifted up the snake in the desert, so *the Son of Man must be lifted up*, that everyone who believes in him may have eternal life." (John 3:14–15, emphasis added)

> "But I, when I am lifted up from the earth, *will draw all men to myself.*" (John 12:32, emphasis added)

> When I came to you, brothers, I did not come with eloquence or superior wisdom as I proclaimed to you the testimony about God. For I resolved to know nothing while I was with you except *Jesus Christ and him crucified.* (1 Corinthians 2:1–2, emphasis added)

> We always carry around in our body the *death of Jesus*, so that the *life of Jesus* may also be revealed in our body. For we who are alive are always being given over to death *for Jesus' sake*, so that *his life* may be revealed in

our mortal body. (2 Corinthians 4:10–11, emphasis added)

But whatever was to my profit I now consider loss *for the sake of Christ.* What is more, I consider everything a loss compared to the surpassing greatness of *knowing Christ Jesus my Lord, for whose sake I have lost all things.* I consider them rubbish, that I may gain Christ. (Philippians 3:7–8, emphasis added)

The person of Jesus himself is motivating. We are to believe in him; we are to feed on him; we are to follow him. "'Come, follow me,' Jesus said, 'and I will make you fishers of men.'" (Mark 1:17). Fishing for men is one of the exciting benefits of following Jesus, but we are first and foremost called to follow him. Christianity is a relationship with God through Jesus Christ, not a program of discipleship, no matter how exciting it may or may not be. As I wrote in the poem that opens this chapter:

Jesus said, "Follow me,
and we'll teach others to follow."
But put the cart before the horse,
and religion will soon be hollow.

If we put the cart before the horse, then we will find our motivation waning over time. But if we keep Jesus in the primary and central role that the Bible gives him, then all of the other motivations in God's word will fall into place around him: faith, hope, love, heaven, pleasing God, judgment, love for others, love of Christ and our mission as his ambassadors. These motivations are only possible because of Jesus Christ. He himself is our primary and ultimate motivation. As Jesus says in the final chapter of the Bible: "Behold, I am coming soon! My reward is with me, and I will give to everyone according to what he has done. I am the Alpha and the Omega, the First and the Last, the Beginning and the End" (Revelation 22:12–13).

I encourage you to go back and read the poem that began this chapter. It articulates the importance of lifting up Jesus and not just telling people what to do, which can lead to legalism and burn-out. Ironically, many people want to be told what to do. But God, in his infinite wisdom, gave us a man to follow, not a program. May we have the courage to follow that man the rest of our lives.

Keep Jesus at the center of your world, and your world will stay centered.

Born to Run

In the day we sweat it out in the streets
of a runaway American dream.
At night we ride through mansions of glory
in suicide machines.

Sprung from cages out on highway 9;
chrome wheeled, fuel injected
and steppin' out over the line.
Baby this town rips the bones from your back
it's a death trap, it's a suicide rap—
we gotta get out while we're young—
'cause tramps like us, baby we were born to run!

The highway's jammed with broken heroes
on a last chance power drive.
Everybody's out on the run tonight
but there's no place left to hide.

Together, Wendy, we can live with the sadness.
I'll love you with all the madness in my soul.
Someday girl, I don't know when,
we're going to get to that place
where we really want to go,
and we'll walk in the sun—
but till then, tramps like us—
baby we were born to run![1]

—Bruce Springsteen

10
BORN TO RUN
Longing for Heaven

Do you feel the hunger deep down in your soul? Usually we keep it contained and quiet, but sometimes it erupts without warning like a red-hot volcano with its burning lava pouring out any way that it can. It is like an untamed animal—wild, restless and ravenous. It is primal and undomesticated, fleshly but not carnal—in fact it is very spiritual. This hunger is desire on fire, burning hot with sensation, drunk with anticipation—but not inherently wrong. It is intoxicating and alluring, stimulating and passionate, ready and willing. It is the call of the wild, a growl in the jungle. It is the seduction of freedom from all that inhibits us. It is the allurement of achievement—bold, gutsy— even audacious! It is an unbridled gallop that courses through the uncharted regions of the imagination. It is an impulsive reaction to the limits of the soul, a desperate conviction that there must be something more. It is a full-tilt race to outrun the mundane, a furious attempt to find the headwaters of meaning. It is torment of the physical, claustrophobia of the spirit! It is a hunger that can't be fully satisfied, an itch that can't be fully scratched—a dream, a wish, a yearning, a hankering, a pining, a languishing, a gasping, a sighing, a crying, a panting and a craving for something more than what this life has to offer! We know somehow we were "born to run." We were made for something better and we know it! We just don't know exactly what it is...

The Bible uses several words to describe this universal phenomenon: "hunger," "thirst," "desire" and others. But the Biblical words that say it best for me are "groaning" and "longing"—the feeling inside of us that groans and longs for something more.

Longing to Be Clothed with Our Heavenly Dwelling

> Now we know that if the earthly tent we live in is destroyed, we have a building from God, an eternal house in heaven, not built by human hands. Meanwhile we *groan*, *longing* to be clothed with our heavenly dwelling, because when we are clothed, we will not be found naked. For while we are in this tent, we *groan* and are burdened, because we do not wish to be unclothed but to be clothed with our heavenly dwelling, so that what is mortal may be swallowed up by life. (2 Corinthians 5:1–4, emphasis added)

Have you ever felt guilty as a Christian because you still felt like you were searching for something more? We are told that the Christian life is fulfilling and satisfying, and then when we feel unfulfilled and unsatisfied as a Christian, we think something is terribly wrong, either with us or with Christianity.

The problem is not with us, or with Christianity. The problem is that we were never taught to "groan" and "long" as Christians. The verse above says that the normal Christian experience is one of groaning and longing. Why? Because we were created for an existential experience that far surpasses the one in this life, and so we are a sports car in first gear, knowing we have the capacity for more, but not able to shift into the higher gears. We mistakenly think that we are only a compact car, meant for basic transportation, when in fact we are that red Ferrari, crafted for speed and excitement beyond our wildest dreams!

We were created for "an eternal house in heaven" (v1), but for now we are living in "an earthly tent" (v1). Haven't you felt that way about your body? This old body of ours keeps breaking down and getting sick and getting in the way; that's because it is a temporary residence—a flimsy tent, designed for camping, not eternity. Imagine if the house you were living in now was actually a tent. Would you feel a little cramped? Would you get irritated at the lack of warmth in the winter and cool in the summer? Would the leaks and bugs and dirt drive you crazy after a while? (Even if you're one of those avid campers, you still wouldn't want to live in a tent permanently, would you?)

That is what the apostle Paul calls our physical bodies—temporary tents, brought along for the journey until we reach our final destination: "an eternal house in heaven, not built by human hands" (v1). Doesn't that explain a lot? Maybe that explains why we are never quite satisfied with our lives, why even the highest highs are still transitory and the deepest fulfillments still fade away. God never promised us heaven on earth—just a better life than before, and the hope of heaven some day.

Oh, don't get me wrong—the Christian life is vastly superior, hugely more satisfying and tons more fulfilling than a worldly life without God. I wake up every morning happy to be with God and so thankful to be right with him. My marriage and family are deeply important to me, and a great source of joy and fulfillment every single day of my life. There is simply no life better than the true Christian life. It is the best life available.

But it is not heaven. It is not what we were ultimately created for. It is not the pot of gold at the end of the rainbow. This is just a pit stop really, on our way to the finish line!

Meanwhile We Groan

So, that makes this whole life "meanwhile." We are waiting for the big show, but *meanwhile* we wait for the show to begin. We are anticipating the grand entrance of the performers, but *meanwhile* we chat with a friend in the next seat. We look forward to the live music, but *meanwhile* there is background music playing over the loud speakers. This is not the show itself—it is just *meanwhile*.

And that makes us groan. Like being stuck in a traffic jam at rush hour when we are eager to get home, we are burdened by the wait. But God is using this time to refine our character, test our faith, and build the anticipation of the big show to come.

> I consider that our present sufferings are not worth comparing with the glory that will be revealed in us. The creation waits in eager expectation for the sons of God to be revealed. For the creation was subjected to frustration, not by its own choice, but by the will of the one who subjected it, in hope that the creation itself will be liberated from its bondage to decay and brought into the glorious freedom of the children of God.
>
> We know that the whole creation has been *groaning* as in the pains of childbirth right up to the present time. Not only so, but we ourselves, who have the first-fruits of the Spirit, *groan* inwardly as we wait eagerly for our adoption as sons, the redemption of our bodies. For in this hope we were saved. But hope that is seen is no hope at all. Who hopes for what he already has? But if we hope for what we do not yet have, we wait for it patiently. (Romans 8:18–25, emphasis added)

The physical universe itself is frustrated and longing for the time when it will be liberated from its own bondage to decay and brought into the freedom of the children of God. That is why the scripture says, "the whole creation has been *groaning* as in the pains of childbirth right up to the present time" (v22, emphasis added). This whole creation includes us, who "*groan* inwardly as we wait eagerly for our adoption as sons, the redemption of our bodies" (v23, emphasis added).

We are pregnant with anticipation, eager for the birth of our renewed bodies, our renewed relationships, and our renewed existence; but uncomfortable nonetheless. It is that mixed feeling of expectant mothers: eager for *the baby* to be born, and eager for the baby *to be born!* (We guys can't relate, but we can imagine.)

So our "meanwhile" is filled with eager anticipation of the

time when we will enjoy the complete redemption that God has begun in us (Ephesians 1:14), but it is also a difficult and painful time that must be endured patiently. "But if we hope for what we do not yet have, we wait for it patiently" (v25).

Notice how the apostle John opens his letter to the church with this thought in the book of Revelation: "I, John, your brother and companion in the suffering and kingdom and patient endurance that are ours in Jesus, was on the island of Patmos because of the word of God and the testimony of Jesus" (Revelation 1:9, emphasis added). John clearly portrays this "patient endurance" as a normal part of the everyday Christian life. Do not fight it; accept it as a part of our lives and a welcome means by which God refines our characters and prepares us for the crescendo of life—heaven itself! (See Romans 5:1–5.)

Longing for a Better Country

> All these people were still living by faith when they died. They did not receive the things promised; they only saw them and welcomed them from a distance. And they admitted that they were aliens and strangers on earth. People who say such things show that they are looking for a country of their own. If they had been thinking of the country they had left, they would have had opportunity to return. Instead, they were *longing* for a better country—a heavenly one. Therefore God is not ashamed to be called their God, for he has prepared a city for them. (Hebrews 11:13–16, emphasis added)

I love that last line: "Therefore God is not ashamed to be called their God, for he has prepared a city for them" (v16). Imagine preparing a big, beautiful banquet for somebody, and then the guests that you invited don't even bother to show up. How would you feel about those people? In the parable of the great banquet, Jesus tells us that the host, representing God, was angry at those who refused to come and declared that none of them would get a taste of his banquet (Luke 14:21, 24).

But the Hebrews 11 verse above is not about those who were

invited and did not show up to the banquet. It is about those who were invited and did come. In fact, they were looking so forward to the heavenly banquet that they were "longing" for it (v16). And that is what pleased God so very much—so much so, that God is not ashamed to be called their God, and he is looking forward to presenting them with a heavenly city that is sure to blow their minds and comfort their souls.

Do you long for heaven? Do you find yourself gazing out the window sometimes just daydreaming about leaving this planet and being perfectly united with God and all your friends in a garden paradise forever? Or do "the worries of this life, the deceitfulness of wealth, and the desire for other things" (Mark 4:19) come into your mind more often and choke the word of God in your heart? God created us to long, to dream for something better—a heavenly country that he has meticulously prepared for us from the beginning of time.

Listen to the words of these songs of longing and let them articulate the hunger of your own soul.

Mercy Lord

In my heart sometimes I ponder,
as down life's road I wander,
to a city over yonder,
where peace and love abide.

Where my trials are gone forever
and my tears will find me never.
You'll see; there'll be
a place for me
when I reach the other side.

I have started for a city
that is free from shame and pity.
It's a bright eternal city
where peace and love abide.

Someday I'll have to leave you.
Do not let my parting grieve you.

You'll see; there'll be
a place for me
and I'm going there someday.

Dear Lord, look down upon me
and Lord have mercy on me.
I am just a weary pilgrim;
I am tired and so forlorn.

I thank you for your blessings
and for all that I'm possessing.
You'll see there'll be
a place for me
and I'm going there some day.

Encourage My Soul

Encourage my soul
and let us journey on,
for the night is dark
and I am far from home.

Thanks be to God
the morning light is near.
The storm is passing over.
Hallelujah.

Our Guarantee of Heaven

Sometimes "hope" gets a bad rap. Somewhere in the back of our minds we wonder if there is any real basis for confidence in the hope that we have, or if it is nothing more than "wishful thinking." God anticipated our need for some concrete evidence for the hope of heaven and so he conceived of a plan whereby when we are baptized for the forgiveness of our sins, we also at that time receive the gift of the Holy Spirit to live inside us (Acts 2:38–39). The Holy Spirit thus lives inside of all true Christians (Romans 8:9).

The Holy Spirit has several roles in our lives, including these: guiding us into all truth (John 16:13), interceding for us during our prayers with groans that words cannot express (Romans 8:26), empowering us to put to death the misdeeds of the body and overcome sin (Romans 8:13), producing the fruits of love, joy, peace, patience, kindness, goodness, faithfulness, gentleness and self-control in our lives (Galatians 5:22), and many others. But one of the key roles of the Holy Spirit is to function as a "deposit, guaranteeing what is to come"—the future blessings of heaven. See this role clearly identified in the following verses:

> He anointed us, set his seal of ownership on us, and put his Spirit in our hearts as a deposit, guaranteeing what is to come. (2 Corinthians 1:22)

> Now it is God who has made us for this very purpose and has given us the Spirit as a deposit, guaranteeing what is to come. (2 Corinthians 5:5)

> And you also were included in Christ when you heard the word of truth, the gospel of your salvation. Having believed, you were marked in him with a seal, the promised Holy Spirit, who is a deposit guaranteeing our inheritance until the redemption of those who are God's possession—to the praise of his glory. (Ephesians 1:13–14)

God has given us a wonderful guarantee of heaven: he has given us his Holy Spirit to live inside of us to produce his fruit, his power and his wisdom in our lives so that we will know there is plenty more where that came from. The Holy Spirit is his pledge that assures us, promises us and guarantees us that we will receive an inheritance from God that will make the riches of this life look like poverty.

What Is It Going to Be Like?

Have you ever wondered what heaven is going to be like? Many of us are embarrassed to admit what we really think about heaven: that it is going to be boring! Go ahead, admit it, you have wondered how in the world you are going to sit through an eternity of prayer and harp music without being bored out of your mind! That is because you have been misinformed about heaven. I assure you that heaven will be anything but boring! In fact, it will be just the opposite.

Here is one author's view of heaven:

> All things will be new: new colors, new sounds, new every-thing. …In heaven, we will discover the depths of all the wis-dom and treasures of God's mind and heart (Colossians 2:2–3). We will be shown the glories and incomparable vast-ness of his creative imagination—maybe even enter it, as in a dream. Perhaps we will be given new creative powers our-selves—powers to compose, to build, or to set out on voyages of discovery—powers worthy of true sons of God. What awaits us is surprise upon surprise…. Every moment will be like having your eyes opened for the very first time. We will experience unfading powers, riches, adventure, pleasures and feasts. Secrets will be uncovered, laws understood, questions answered, mysteries made known. We will never say, "'What else is there to do here?" The glory will never diminish, never bore us even for a moment.[2]

Wow, that's exciting! And why wouldn't it be? God conceived of us and created us for the express purpose of being with him and each other in heaven for eternity. Doesn't it make sense that heaven would feel right to us, like hand in glove, key in lock? More beautiful than the most gorgeous mountain landscapes, more enjoyable than a dream vacation in Hawaii, and more sat-isfying than the most precious and intimate moments shared with loved ones here on earth—heaven will be infinitely better than all of that! God guarantees it!

> Then I saw a new heaven and a new earth, for the first heaven and the first earth had passed away, and there was no longer any sea. I saw the Holy City, the new Jerusalem, coming down out of heaven from God, pre-pared as a bride beautifully dressed for her husband. And I heard a loud voice from the throne saying, "Now the dwelling of God is with men, and he will live with them.

> They will be his people, and God himself will be with them and be their God. He will wipe every tear from their eyes. There will be no more death or mourning or crying or pain, for the old order of things has passed away."
> (Revelation 21:1–4)

Just imagine: "He will wipe every tear from their eyes. There will be no more death or mourning or crying or pain, for the old order of things has passed away" (v4). All past hurts will be healed as "the Father of compassion and the God of all comfort" (2 Corinthians 1:3) personally wipes every tear from the eyes of each one of us with the loving compassion of he who is love incarnate (1 John 4:16).

But there is more.

We Shall Behold Him

As amazing as all of this will be, there is still one more thing that I am looking forward to about heaven that we have not yet mentioned specifically. But let me tell you a story first.

I love to go on prayer walks with God. It is my favorite thing to do. I particularly enjoy walking around lakes or parks or other picturesque settings that breathe life and beauty into my soul. On one of those prayer walks many years ago I had an unforgettable conversation with God. It went something like this. I told God: "I love being with you, God. I really enjoy reading your incredible word and praying to you and singing you my favorite songs and listening to you speak to me through your Spirit and just hanging out with you. But I have a request: I want to see you. I want to see your face. I want to look into your eyes and have you look back at me. I want to connect on that level. After all, I talk to you all the time, and I feel like we have a great relationship, but I don't even know what you look like. I can only imagine. I want to look into the eyes that peer deep down into my soul—and smile. I want to see the brilliant face of the one who said, "Let there be light!" and billions upon billions of stars the size of the sun were born! I want to gaze at the one who came up with a plan to make creatures in his own magnificent image, knowing they would sin and ruin that image, and then predestine that he would give his only begotten Son to die for them so that they would know just how much he loves them. I want to know the face of the one who heard me cry out at the lowest point of my life and bent down to scoop me up in his hands and place me back on solid ground, and has saved me over and over again since then, so many times. I want to know you like you know me. Please God, grant me one wish: I just want to see you and the look on your face when you look at me."

After my sincere prayer, I waited with baited breath to see him appear. After all, Jesus promised us we would receive whatever we ask for in prayer, right? (Matthew 21:22). So, I waited, and waited and waited. But he did not show himself to me. (Are you laughing?) I wasn't. In fact, I was crying so hard I began to sob and sob. I did not understand why he would not do for me this one small favor that I knew he could do easily. But he did not do it, though I am sure to this day that he was dying to rip through whatever dimensions separate us and come to me to comfort the son that he loves more dearly than I love any of my own three children.

And then I saw it in God's word…that very special and intimate moment is reserved for heaven:

> They will see his face, and his name will be on their foreheads. (Revelation 22:4)

> Now we see but a poor reflection as in a mirror; then we shall see face to face. Now I know in part; then I shall know fully, even as I am fully known. (1 Corinthians 13:12)

> And I—in righteousness I will see your face;
>   when I awake, I will be satisfied with seeing your
>   likeness. (Psalm 17:15)

I realized that God is reserving this very prized and cherished moment for a very special time that has not yet arrived. He knows what he is doing. He is saving it for when the time is right. And I will be ready. In fact, I will be primed with anticipation because I have looked so forward to it. This must be how the Psalmist felt when he wrote the longing prayer of Psalm 42:

> As the deer pants for streams of water,
>   so my soul pants for you, O God.
> My soul thirsts for God, for the living God.
>   When can I go and meet with God? (Psalm 42:1–2)

Can you relate to this Psalm? I know many of you can, and if you can't quite yet, God will be patient with you and help you get there. This type of longing is not unique; it is the longing of thirsty souls in the desert since the beginning of time. Like us, our God wants to be wanted, he desires to be desired, and he longs to be longed for.

I wrote the following piece a few years ago. I hope it increases your own yearning for God.

His Face

I know what I want.
That's what happens when you get older—you begin to eliminate
*   options.*
The more mistakes you make, the more options you begin to elimi-
*   nate,*
until your focus becomes narrowed, and then, in one magical
*   moment,*
that focus becomes singular.

Clarity of purpose produces incredible energy.
A man who knows what he wants will stop at nothing to get it.
His hunger becomes selective and intensifies.
Do you know what you want?
What will you stop at nothing to get?
What are you hungry for?

I know what I want.
I want to see God's face.

When it's just he and I together, all alone, just the two of us.
I want to see him.
I like to read about him and I like to hear about him.
But I long to see him, to look into his eyes as he looks back at me,
and to know him, as he knows me.

That's what I want. He knows that. I've told him several times.
Many times when it's just been he and I together in one of our
favorite prayer spots
I've begged him: "Come on, just once, just let me see you."
And he wanted to do it. Even now he longs to show himself to me.
In fact, I believe it kills him to have to hold back!
But he doesn't do it. He won't do it. He won't show me his face.
Even though he longs to do it.
And I long to see it.

But that just makes our desire increase.
One day, one very special and glorious day, he will do it.
He will reveal himself to me—
and I will see him—face to face.
I long for that day.
I live for that day—
when I shall behold him, face to face…

—Jeff Chacon

We Shall Overcome

But we have to make it to heaven to see God. And our enemy, the devil, who opposes us at every step along the way (Revelation 12:17), will not make it easy. We've got to fight, we've got to toil, and we've got to do whatever it takes to make it to the very end! But, just remember this one thing: it will be totally worth it!

Listen to Paul's personal testimony about his life in probably one of the very last letters that he wrote:

> For I am already being poured out like a drink offering, and the time has come for my departure. I have fought the good fight, I have finished the race, I have kept the faith. Now there is in store for me the crown of right-eousness, which the Lord, the righteous Judge, will

award to me on that day—and not only to me, but also to all who have longed for his appearing. (2 Timothy 4:6-8)

That's how I want to go out; that's how I want to finish my life; that's how I want to hear the final bell—confident that I have remained faithful to God, still standing in the middle of the boxing ring. I might be bloody and sweating, but not beaten, and I will be ready to receive "the crown of righteousness, which the Lord, the righteous Judge, will award to me on that day—and not only to me, but also to all who have *longed* for his appearing" (v8, emphasis added).

Listen to God cheering us on with his promises from the book of Revelation that urge us to make it to the very end and overcome.

"He who has an ear, let him hear what the Spirit says to the churches. To him who *overcomes*, I will give the right to eat from the tree of life, which is in the paradise of God." (Revelation 2:7, emphasis added)

"He who has an ear, let him hear what the Spirit says to the churches. He who *overcomes* will not be hurt at all by the second death." (Revelation 2:11, emphasis added)

"He who has an ear, let him hear what the Spirit says to the churches. To him who *overcomes*, I will give some of the hidden manna. I will also give him a white stone with a new name written on it, known only to him who receives it." (Revelation 2:17, emphasis added)

"To him who *overcomes* and does my will to the end, I will give authority over the nations—

'He will rule them with an iron scepter;
he will dash them to pieces like pottery'—

just as I have received authority from my Father. I will also give him the morning star. He who has an ear, let him hear what the Spirit says to the churches." (Revelation 2:26-29, emphasis added)

"Yet you have a few people in Sardis who have not soiled their clothes. They will walk with me, dressed in white, for they are worthy. He who *overcomes* will, like them, be dressed in white. I will never blot out his name from the book of life, but will acknowledge his name before my Father and his angels. He who has an ear, let him hear what the Spirit says to the churches." (Revelation 3:4–6, emphasis added)

"I am coming soon. Hold on to what you have, so that no one will take your crown. Him who *overcomes* I will make a pillar in the temple of my God. Never again will he leave it. I will write on him the name of my God and the name of the city of my God, the new Jerusalem, which is coming down out of heaven from my God; and I will also write on him my new name. He who has an ear, let him hear what the Spirit says to the churches." (Revelation 3:11–13, emphasis added)

"To him who *overcomes*, I will give the right to sit with me on my throne, just as I overcame and sat down with my Father on his throne. He who has an ear, let him hear what the Spirit says to the churches." (Revelation 3:21–22, emphasis added)

I don't know about you, but I want to "eat from the tree of life that is in the paradise of God"; I don't want to "be hurt at all by the second death"; I want "some of the hidden manna," and a white stone with my new, secret name on it. I want to rule the nations with an iron scepter and receive the Morning Star (Revelation 2:26–28). Whatever that means—it sure sounds great to me! I want my name to never be blotted out of the book of life, and to have my name acknowledged by Jesus before God and his angels; I want God and Jesus and the Holy City's name written on me, never to be washed away because that is my new home forever; and I want to be given the right to sit on Jesus' throne and rule with him for eternity.

Dare to Dream Again

Is that what you want? Do you know what you want? Is there anything you could possibly dare to dream that would be any more bold, ambitious and stirring than this dream of God for your life? Then go get it! Reach out and grab it! Dare to believe that it could be yours! Dare to get up and try again! Dare to say no to the shackles of sin that have held you down for far too long! Dare to defy the voice of Satan, screaming in your ear: "You can't do it! You'll only fail again! You're a loser and a hypocrite!" Dare to believe the promises of God: "You can do it! You haven't failed until you fail to get up again! You're a winner, a true child of God with a great destiny and inheritance!" Dare to listen to the voice of God, singing his songs of love and belief in you! Dare to defy the critics, "whose cold and timid souls know neither victory nor defeat." Dare to believe that you can follow in the footsteps of great men and women of faith in the Bible who got knocked down, but not knocked out. Dare to remember who you really are and the new name that God has called you by faith!

Hang on! He is coming soon! Don't let anyone take your crown. Don't let anyone take your name. And don't let anyone take your dreams. Whatever you have been through, however many times you have failed, I beg you—dare to dream again!

NOTES

Chapter 1: Look to the Sky!

1. D. H. Groberg, "The Race." © D. H. Goldberg. All rights reserved. Reprinted by permission.

Chapter 2: Hiding in Caves

1. Music by Claude-Michel Schönberg. Lyrics by Alan Boublil, Herbert Kretzmer, Jean Claude Lucchetti Mourou and Claude-Michel Schonberg, "I Dreamed a Dream." © 1980 Editions Musicales Alain Boublil. All rights reserved. Reprinted by permission.

2. Scott Michael Cutler, Anne Preven and Philip Carden, "Torn." © 1995, 1996 BMG Music Publishing Ltd; Colgems-EMI Music Inc., Scott Cutler Music; Universal-Songs of PolyGram International, Inc. and Weetie-Pie Music. All rights reserved. Reprinted by permission.

3. Bill Berry, Peter Buck, Mike Mills and Michael Stipe, "Everybody Hurts." © 1992 Night Garden Music. All rights reserved. Reprinted by permission.

Chapter 3: What If I Were to Tell You

1. This is a favorite saying of Mike Rock, evangelist for the Jacksonville Church of Christ.

2. Marsha J. Stevens, "For Those Tears I Died." © 1969 Bud John Songs, Inc. (ASCAP). Administered by EMI Christian Music Publishing. All rights reserved. Reprinted by permission.

Chapter 4: It's All About Love

1. The Bible's teaching on our purpose and mission in life is actually much more complex and multifaceted than this and has only been simplified here for emphasis.

2. I. B. Sergai,"My God and I." © 1935 Singspiration Music

(ASCAP). Administered by Brentwood-Benson Music Publishing, Inc. All rights reserved. Reprinted by permission.

Chapter 7: Faith at the Door

1. Through the years tradition has connected Mary Magdaline with the sinful woman who washed Jesus' feet. However, the Scriptures never make this identification. Therefore, this account is only a conjecture.

Chapter 8: Standing on the Promises

1. Music by Andrew Lloyd Webber. Lyrics by Charles Hart. Additional Lyrics by Richard Stilgoe, "All I Ask of You." © 1986 The Really Useful Group Ltd. All rights reserved. Reprinted by permission.

Chapter 10: Born to Run

1. Bruce Springsteen, "Born to Run." © 1975 Bruce Springsteen. All rights reserved. Reprinted by permission.

2. Henry Kriete, *Worship the King*, (Billerica, Mass.: Discipleship Publications International, 2000), 206.